TS-191

HANDBOOK OF
LORIES & LORIKEETS

ROGER SWEENEY

Handbook of Lories & Lorikeets

Ornate Lorikeet, *Trichoglossus ornatus*.

View of the gardens and aviary at Birdworld Bird Park in Surrey, England.

Title page: Pair of Chattering Lories *Lorius garrulus flavopalliatus*.

Photographs: David Alderton; Gerald Allen; Mary Andrews; Dr. Herbert R. Axelrod; courtesy of Bird Depot, Inc.; G. Bouchier; Thomas Brosset; Alwin Clements; D. Coles; Michael DeFreitas; Harry Frauca; R. H. Grantham; Ray Hanson; Fred Harris; M. Heidenreich; courtesy of Dr. F. W. Huchzermeyer; P. Leysen; courtesy of Midori Shobo; Irene & Michael Morcombe; Robert Pearcy; Fritz Prenzel; K. Price; Elaine Radford; L. Robinson; courtesy of San Diego Zoo; R. Sweeney; Tony Tilford; courtesy of Vogelpark Walsrode; C. Wright.
Drawings: John Quinn.

t.f.h.

Distributed in the UNITED STATES to the Pet Trade by T.F.H. Publications, Inc., One T.F.H. Plaza, Neptune City, NJ 07753; distributed in the UNITED STATES to the Bookstore and Library Trade by National Book Network, Inc. 4720 Boston Way, Lanham MD 20706; in CANADA to the Pet Trade by H & L Pet Supplies Inc., 27 Kingston Crescent, Kitchener, Ontario N2B 2T6; Rolf C. Hagen Ltd., 3225 Sartelon Street, Montreal 382 Quebec; in CANADA to the Book Trade by Macmillan of Canada (A Division of Canada Publishing Corporation), 164 Commander Boulevard, Agincourt, Ontario M1S 3C7; in ENGLAND by T.F.H. Publications, PO Box 15, Waterlooville PO7 6BQ; in AUSTRALIA AND THE SOUTH PACIFIC by T.F.H. (Australia), Pty. Ltd., Box 149, Brookvale 2100 N.S.W., Australia; in NEW ZEALAND by Brooklands Aquarium Ltd. 5 McGiven Drive, New Plymouth, RD1 New Zealand; in the PHILIPPINES by Bio-Research, 5 Lippay Street, San Lorenzo Village, Makati, Rizal; in SOUTH AFRICA by Multipet Pty. Ltd., P.O. Box 35347, Northway, 4065, South Africa. Published by T.F.H. Publications, Inc. Manufactured in the United States of America by T.F.H. Publications, Inc.

Contents

Acknowledgements

This book would not have been possible without the help of many people, but mainly I would like to thank the following: David Harvey for his help and advice while writing this book; Keith Mitchell for help and information given; David Coles for help and information plus the use of photographs; Cliff Wright for help and the use of photographs; Rob Harvey for help and incubation advice; Gavin Bourchier and Charles Deeming for assistance and help with photographs; Simon Joshua of Databird Worldwide Scientific Services for information and the use of the photograph to illustrate blood-feather sexing; and Kate Price for photographs.

ROGER SWEENEY

Main entrance to the aviaries at Birdworld, where the author was in charge of lory management.

Violet-naped Lory, *Eos squamata*.

Introduction

Lories and lorikeets are, in the opinion of many bird keepers, among the most beautifully colored of all bird families. Their rich, vivid colors range from bright scarlet, deep purple and glossy black through to bright lemon yellow, light greens and oranges. When in good health they always look glossy and shine in sunlight, and these striking colors combined with the birds' individuality and personalities mean that once kept they often become firm favorites among aviculturists.

Some doubts still persist in the minds of many new bird keepers about how difficult lories are to keep. Although they are indeed specialized feeders, better understanding of their dietary needs and many new manufactured artificial food products mean that they are as easy, if not easier, to care for than any other group of birds. There is however at the time of this writing a surprising lack of literature available on the subject, which belies the huge interest and large following this group of birds has among bird keepers around the world. In fact, during conversations with members of the public visiting Birdworld and especially during the Avicultural Days organized each year, this subject is one of the most popular talks and perhaps occasions more questions than any other. It was as a result of this huge interest that I started to write this book primarily as a guide to novices who may otherwise be put off, and to try and answer most of the most commonly asked questions on their care and breeding.

A large number of the questions asked usually relate to the diet and the meaning of terms such as "brush-tongued parrot." In the wild, lories and lorikeets feed mainly on pollen and nectar, with some fruit also being taken. To help them harvest nectar and particularly pollen, the papillae on the tip of the tongue are elongated, giving the tip of the tongue a brushlike appearance. The upper mandible is also narrower and more elongated than in other parrots of a similar size. In captivity, however, the main part of the diet is based on an artificial nectar which can be bought or made up from a mixture of glucose, baby milk and honey. In other respects their care does not vary greatly from other more widely kept parrots, and they are among the most prolific breeders. Most species only have two eggs in a clutch but will often have three or even more clutches a year. Some very prolific pairs will even nest through the winter months, although in such cases young chicks can become chilled after the first couple of weeks when the parent birds begin to leave them for longer periods in the brooding. In these cases it may be better to pull the chicks and attempt to hand-rear them.

Little Lorikeets, *Glossopsitta pusilla*, in an aviary. Of the three species in this genus, this native of Australia is the least well-established in captivity.

As a last point of this introduction I cannot overemphasize the importance of trying to breed the birds that you are keeping. As importations of birds from the wild inevitably decrease, it is important to establish strong captive populations of many of the rarer species. In the case of a rare species that is not well established, every individual bird kept in captivity has great importance in maintaining a strong gene pool to ensure the future of its species for many further generations. It is not enough to own one prolific pair and have other unpaired birds, as this leads to the genes of the unproductive pair possibly being wasted forever and reducing the future genetic health of the captive population. Indeed, rather than needing to obtain fresh blood from the wild to maintain the health of a captive population, it may well become the case that captive-bred birds will need to be released to keep the wild populations from becoming isolated and inbred in the not-too-distant future. Indonesia, New Guinea and the surrounding islands, which represent the homes of many species, are among the most threatened countries in the world from deforestation, and the consequences are clear. In the late 1980s many species of lories and lorikeets that have not been seen in aviculture for some time have become available in reasonable numbers, so there is an opportunity to establish these birds in healthy captive populations. Or we risk losing them from aviculture forever.

Lories in the San Diego Zoo. Famed for its large collection of lory species, it was also one of the first zoos to undertake captive breeding programs.

Varied Lorikeet, *Trichoglossus versicolor*.

Obtaining and Initial Care

Choosing New Birds

A majority of lories and lorikeets for sale at the time of this writing are wild-caught birds; this however is gradually changing, with captive-bred birds of most species now becoming available. The advantages of captive-bred birds over wild-caught ones are clear. Captive-bred birds are steadier and more tolerant of being disturbed in the aviary; this point is particularly important if it is intended to breed from the birds. Captive-bred birds are less likely to be afflicted with common parasitic and bacterial problems that so often accompany birds that have been imported from the wild (not always with obvious signs at the time of purchase). Nor are they usually suffering from bad feathering, missing toes or other physical injuries that often occur while being captured and transported from the wild.

Acquiring captive-bred birds can be done either through an established bird dealer or direct from a breeder who can normally be contacted through adverts in various avicultural magazines or through avicultural societies. For anyone new to bird keeping I would strongly suggest the latter course, as acquiring birds directly from a breeder provides a novice with the perfect opportunity to gain first-hand information and advice from a breeder who has bred the species that you are buying. Also, asking about the diet that the birds have been reared on and are used to can reduce stress and problems that can occur when birds are transferred and given a different diet than they are used to without a transition period.

With some species which are only now becoming established in captivity it may be hard to obtain captive-bred stock, so it may be a case of buying wild-caught birds. Lories and lorikeets as a general rule stand up to the rigors of importation better than most groups of birds, although it is in such cases important to be more careful in selecting the birds that you are acquiring. A novice must never be tempted into buying a bird that obviously looks unwell. This of course may sound like a simple statement, but in the case of a particularly rare bird, especially if the dealer offers a large discount or a money-back guarantee, the temptation to take the bird and to try to nurse it back to health can be overwhelming. This temptation should always be

Careful visual inspection for good health is an important part of lory selection. This Musk Lorikeet, *Glossopsitta concinna*, is in good feather.

strongly resisted unless you have adequate quarantine facilities for such an occasion, as consideration should always be given to birds already being kept in your care, which may suffer from the arrival of an unhealthy newcomer to the collection.

Whether the birds you intend to buy are captive bred or wild caught, the following steps should be taken into account when selecting them.

Firstly, when inspecting a bird, particularly one in a cage that is below eye level, do not approach it too quickly. A nervous bird suddenly confronted by a stranger will instinctively tighten its body posture, become more alert and quicken its breathing—all of which on a quick inspection can mislead as to its true state of health. The birds should first be observed from several feet away and approached once they have been observed for several minutes.

Body posture: A healthy bird should be lively, alert and aware of what is happening in the room around it. It should have an alert, upright posture, with a tight stomach and the head held high. The bird should be sure footed when moving around the cage or while perching at rest. A bird in poorer health will firm up its body posture if aware of a stranger watching, but if viewed quietly for a couple of minutes it will start to drop its gut, droop its wings and while at rest will appear to be less sure of its perching, flexing its claws and moving its weight from one foot to another unsurely.

Physical condition: The bird's eyes should be clear and wide open, with no swelling on either the upper or lower eyelids. The feathers should be clean and in good condition, especially if there is bathing water present in the holding cage. The underside of the tail feathers should be given

particular attention to ensure that they are clean and free of the excretion which is often a sign of disease. The body shape should be smooth and not contain any unexplained contours, which may conceal a swelling or past injury. The legs and feet should be inspected for missing claws, cuts or grazes.

Breathing: A bird being viewed closely will instinctively quicken its breathing. This is not a bad sign and even makes it easier to listen for any sound which may indicate a blockage or the presence of liquid in the respiratory passages. The nostrils should also be checked to ensure that they are clear, with no discharge present.

Finally, as the bird is being caught, two last inspections should be made. The breast should be felt to ensure that there is a reasonable amount of fat covering the rib case and the vent should be checked to make sure that it is not blocked and that the undertail feathers are not heavily stained with excretion, which obviously points towards ill health. These final inspections are of great importance and only take moments to do as the bird is being caught. No reasonable dealer or aviculturist should refuse to allow them.

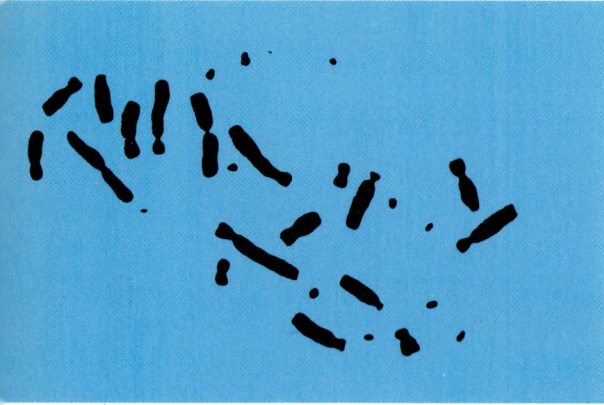

Chromosomes of a female Rainbow Lorikeet. Of the total number of 58 for this species, 18 are the larger macrochromosomes, which are clearly visible.

Sexing Birds

Most of the more commonly available species of lories and lorikeets cannot be sexed visually. Many shipments of wild-caught birds are surgically sexed before being offered for sale, in which case selecting a true pair of birds is not a problem. In many cases, however, it is necessary to try to ascertain the sex of a bird or birds if a serious attempt to breed them is to be made. In the past this has been done by observation of the birds' behavior and slight physical differences; this proved a very haphazard affair even when done by experienced aviculturists. The advent of surgical sexing of birds has been one of the greatest milestones in avicultural history. In the past, species of birds became available in limited numbers and were successfully kept and bred; however, in monomorphic species these breedings were often limited by incorrect sexing, and in those cases where there was success it was subsequently difficult to find unrelated blood and, once found, the sexes had to be guessed at, making a second chance for a mistake to be made.

It is not then surprising that species of birds which arrived in numbers, and were even successfully kept, in the long term failed to become established in aviculture.

Today, with the accurate sexing techniques available and improved understanding of husbandry requirements, most species breed readily. It is important not to rely completely on test results in choosing which birds to pair up. I have always found that the most prolific pair of birds are those which have been allowed to choose their own mates. Once birds have been sexed, a temporary marking agent can be used to mark all the males or all the females on the back or tail feathers. Some vets use a marking agent on the legs of birds they have just sexed. This means that the birds can then be placed together in a large flight to enable them to choose their own mates. A close watch should be kept to prevent any fighting breaking out and to ensure two birds of the same sex do not try to pair up. True pairs should be removed once they demonstrate evidence of a pair bond, and in the rare cases when two birds of the same sex pair up (usually two males) they should be separated and housed on their own until a bird of the opposite sex becomes available to pair with. Such birds, once paired to a correct mate, will go on to breed successfully.

Sexing by physical characteristics and behavior: In many species there is no obvious color or physical difference between the sexes and it is necessary to look for more subtle signs to indicate sex. In male birds the upper mandible is sometimes slightly larger and broader at the base; also, the bridge of the skull is slightly higher above the eye than in the female. Sexing by behavior is even more difficult. Two males which are housed together will show signs of dominance and recessiveness which can be almost indistinguishable from the behavior of a true pair.

Surgical sexing via laparoscope: This technique involves anaesthesia of the bird and uses a laparoscope, which is a long, thin, hollow surgical probe containing a fiber-optic cable which, once inserted, allows the interior view to be seen through an eyepiece at the external end. The laparoscope is uscd for all manner of avian medicine but for sexing it is inserted into the left abdominal air sac to view the gonads.

The testicles of the male are elliptical in shape, with blood vessels traversing the smooth surface. The testicles are paired, although normally only one is visible, and they may vary in size through the year, depending on the breeding cycle of the bird. The ovary, by comparison, has grapelike clusters of prominent follicles and is easy to distinguish from the male organs.

The main problem of surgical sexing is the risk involved with anesthetizing the bird. Many captive birds which may have lived quite healthily for a number of years may even so be carrying dormant infections, such as avian tuberculosis, which can be triggered by stress. This is especially worrying if the bird has to be caught up and transported to the place of the operation over a number of hours. It is normal not to allow the bird access to food for a number of hours prior to sexing to allow the digestive tract to clear.

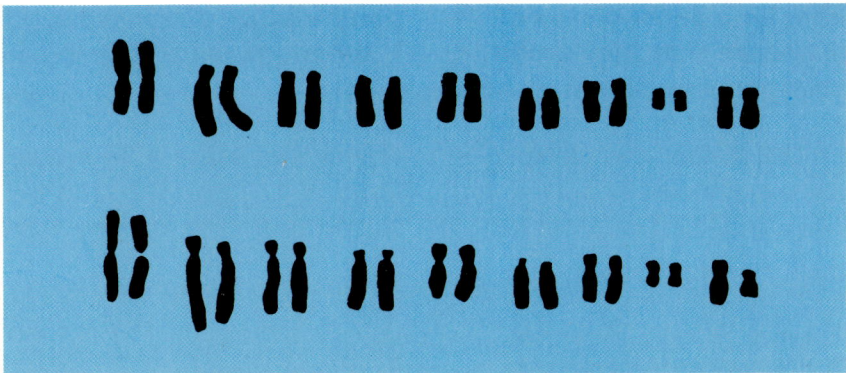

Chromosomes of male (upper row) and female (lower row) Rainbow Lorikeets. With the sex chromosomes placed last in the rows, the male is indicated by a pair of similar-sized Z chromosomes, while in the female the single Z chromosome is accompanied by the smaller W chromosome.

Blood-feather sexing: This is the most recent and by far the best technique for sexing birds, although it is only just becoming widely available. This technique can be carried out on any bird over six weeks of age and has the advantage of not requiring the bird to be anesthetized or operated on. Instead, a blood feather is pulled as it grows through and is placed in a sealed tube. This is sent to a laboratory where chromosomes are extracted from the blood-feather pulp and examined, as there are clear differences between the chromosomes of male and female birds. If you are not aware of any place local that offers this service, then it is well worth contacting a local zoo or bird garden, which may be of help to you. Samples can be stored for some time in a frozen state, so it may be possible for several people to store and send in batches together.

Quarantining New Birds

In most cases when new birds are obtained, it is best to quarantine them for a short period of time to ensure that they are fit and healthy before allowing them outside and to come into contact with established birds. Quarantine cages should be in a warm, draftfree and frostfree room, although in the case of birds which are already acclimatized it is best not to give them too much heat, as this may prove counterproductive and delay their return to an outside aviary. Most newly imported birds will usually benefit from a background temperature of around 24° C, particularly smaller, more delicate species such as the Fairy Lorikeet (*Charmosyna pulchella*). Cleanliness is essential when birds are in confinement, as lories are especially messy, with excretion being sprayed out through the sides of the cage as well as onto the cage floor. For this reason I have found the ideal quarantine cage to be an all-wire cage suspended from either the wall or ceiling in a room with all the walls and floor of the room being covered with easy-to-clean tiles. The individual cages should contain a shallow water dish to enable the birds to bathe; if this is not possible, then the birds will benefit from a light spraying daily with lukewarm water. If hanging cages cannot be used, then any parakeet-proof cage will do, but remember to have plenty of newspaper surrounding the cage so that any excretion falling outside the cage does not stain the furniture. If a cage with solid sides is used, then the inside walls should receive regular cleaning to prevent excretion building up on them.

When keeping birds in confinement inside it is also important to ensure that there is adequate ventilation, especially in warm summer months. If a room contains more than one bird cage and has a window which will open outwards, then it would be a good idea to construct a wire frame which can hang on the inside of the window frame when the window is open and so help reduce any risk of escape should a bird manage to escape from its cage.

As well as allowing the keeper to look more closely for any possible signs that indicate poor health, a quarantine period often allows the bird to become much steadier in the presence of its owner. It also allows for a close watch to be kept to make sure that the bird is eating properly and not just spilling its food out of the cage, especially if the diet it is receiving is slightly different from what it received before. Food and water dishes should always be hung next to perches so that the bird can reach them with a minimum of effort. This may seem a trivial point if the bird is confined to a fairly small cage, but it is surprising the amount of difference this can make to a bird which is unsure and not especially interested in food other than picking at it out of boredom.

Once the keeper is satisfied that the bird is in good health and is feeding well, then it is simply a case of waiting for suitable weather to introduce the bird to an outside aviary. Before this is done is often an opportune time to worm the bird. Ideally if two birds are to be paired up, then they should both be introduced to the aviary at the same time. If one bird is already present in the aviary, then it may well be a wise precaution to remove it for a couple of days and allow the new bird to familiarize itself with the aviary before the original bird is reintroduced. Birds if possible should be allowed out in late spring or early summer, but mainly when the weather is warm and there is not too much rain or

Aviary-kept Chattering Lory, *Lorius garrulus*, preening itself—this is a sign of well-being, as ill birds do not have energy to spare on caring for their plumage.

cold wind that might chill the bird. Care should be taken to make sure the bird can find its food easily, and if in any doubt it is probably best to lock the bird away in a draft-proof (but not heated) shelter for the first few nights.

Chattering Lory, *Lorius garrulus*, in a outdoor aviary.

Housing

The housing of the birds you are thinking of obtaining should of course be your first consideration before purchasing them. Most species of lories and lorikeets are best housed in outside aviaries, although these should have frostfree shelters where the birds can be locked away in extreme weather conditions. Introducing birds to an outside aviary should also be done with care. Birds should not be put outside if they are thin, in bad feathering or if they show any signs of ill health or general weakness. The smaller, more delicate lorikeet species should be housed in very sheltered aviaries with protection from unduly strong or cold crosswinds. Some, such as the Fairy Lorikeet (*Charmosyna pulchella*), will fare best in a tropical house if one is available. Otherwise the best way to maintain them is in inside breeding aviaries, which have proved highly successful for the Fairy Lorikeet and other species such as the Red-flanked (*Charmosyna placentis*) and the Goldie's (*Trichoglossus goldiei*) lorikeets. These were previously thought of as being delicate and difficult to keep, yet they will often prove prolific breeders under such circumstances.

Inside Breeding Cages

Inside breeding cages for lorikeets are usually all-wire structures which are suspended from the wall or ceiling in a room where all the walls and floor can be scrubbed down daily. In the case of hobbyists, more often a converted large double Budgie breeding cage can be used. The presence of a solid back and sides to the cage will save spoiling the furniture the cage is resting on, but the interior walls will require regular cleaning. If excretion is allowed to build up on them, they will prove a perfect breeding ground for bacteria. Whether the cages are all wire or have solid sides, the floor should receive regular attention, being scrubbed daily and with any dropped food items being removed as soon as possible. The perches should also be cleaned regularly and replaced once all the bark has been chewed off by the birds. In confinement it is important for the birds to have access to chewing material in order that they keep their bills and claws in good condition. It also helps to prevent problems such as feather plucking, which can be triggered by boredom.

Wherever possible the cage should be serviced without actually entering it. Food and water can be replaced through areas specially cut in the wire, and the nest box should be situated on the outside of the cage so that it can be serviced from the back without actually entering the cage itself. The importance of this point is that birds kept in open cages will initially feel very nervous and exposed, but once they realize that the keeper very rarely enters the actual cage then they become more confident in the cage perimeters and after a while they may even feel more secure in a breeding cage than in an aviary which is being entered every day.

The advantages of using inside cages are, first, that it may allow the keeping of species considered too delicate to be housed outside. Second, the birds are at no risk from predators such as foxes and cats that can cause problems in an outside aviary. Also, there is less environmental disturbance such as traffic or neighbors.

The all-wire parrot cage is suitable for lories; the major drawback is that its surroundings will need constant cleaning.

Finally, the steady temperature and ideal conditions indoors may well lead to increased breeding by the birds, which will some times continue breeding right through the winter.

The only disadvantages to using inside breeding cages come from the birds not being exposed to natural elements such as the sun and rain, which may lead to the birds' feathering becoming tatty. If the inside room in which they're housed is not ventilated adequately, it can become very dry. Provision of good ventilation, bathing water or regular spraying will usually prevent any such problems. The other possible disadvantage is the increased possibility of disease. If a number of birds are kept enclosed in a room, strict cleaning and good ventilation will again minimize such risks occurring.

Aviaries

The first consideration when deciding where to situate the aviary is positioning it with regard to sunlight. An easterly facing aviary will catch more sun in the morning to warm the birds after a cold night. While a well-lit aviary is more attractive and allows the birds to show off their glossy plumage to best effect, the aviary should provide cover and shade for nervous birds, particularly if these are normally forest-dwelling species which have recently been imported. To this effect the sides and roof of the aviary should be covered towards the back, which will also afford some protection against the weather. With smaller

Large cages offer the benefit of room to fly, as well as more flexibility in placing perches, nest boxes, and such.

species it should also be possible to have some bushes and shrubs in the aviary which are big enough to give some cover and not suffer too much from chewing by the birds. Even if the aviary is in a sheltered position, some form of shelter should also be incorporated, especially in countries such as England where the weather is so unpredictable.

Larger lories such as those of genus *Chalcopsitta* may not need a shelter, as they have a habit of roosting in nest boxes, which are normally placed in a sheltered position. In most cases though it is wise when constructing an aviary to include a covered shelter which can be about 100cm long by 40cm wide by 40cm high. The entrance should be via a hole just bigger than the size of the lory itself and should have a flap to cover it for occasions when the birds are to be locked away. This should be placed off the ground in one of the top corners at the back of the aviary. It will also serve another purpose as somewhere to place the food dish where it cannot be reached by mice and not contaminated through the wire by other birds. When locking the birds in at night during periods of bad weather, the birds will soon become used to seeing the net towards the end of the day and will usually fly straight into the shelter with the minimum of encouragement from the keeper.

For wire to cover the aviary I would strongly recommend Twilweld wire, which prevents any injuries to the bird from flying into it and cutting its crown or cere as so commonly happens with chicken wire or other cheap kinds of wire. The size of the wire should be one inch by one-half inch. Although slightly larger wire

could be used without risk of escape by the birds, it may allow pests such as mice or small birds to squeeze through the wire and contaminate food and water provided for the captive birds. I would also recommend that any wire used should be coated with a black bitumen-based paint which not only protects the wire against the elements but also improves the view into the aviary. This is of particular benefit to anyone trying to take photographs through the wire.

The simple addition of a safety door fitted around the main door will prevent any risk of escapes and is well worth installing. In a row of aviaries only one needs to be fitted at the end, then if access is through other aviaries the whole block can be serviced without any chance of a bird escaping completely.

The floor of the aviary should be the next consideration. If the aviary is a reasonably large size and contains just one pair of

Another view of the Birdworld aviary complex.

birds, then there is no reason that grass cannot be used as a base. One pair of birds in a reasonable area is not likely to produce enough excretion so that it would become a hygiene hazard, particularly as the excretion of lories and lorikeets is in such a liquid form anyway. In countries such as England you can always rely on the weather to help break down waste. This does not mean that the rest of the aviary doesn't need cleaning. Any paths and perches should be cleaned regularly, particularly under the places where the lories perch most frequently.

If the aviaries are not so large as to allow this and there is more than one in a row, then an easier-to-clean substrate will be a better covering for the floor. Sand if used should be at a depth of at least ten to fifteen centimeters in order that it can be raked over frequently, which not only gives better hygiene but gives the aviaries a neat, well-maintained appearance. If the ground that the aviary is built on has good drainage then a similar depth of gravel can be used; as well as being raked over, this can also be hosed down to help break down waste. The shelter or wherever the food is placed should be the subject of regular cleaning. It should be cleaned daily if possible, with sawdust proving an ideal base which is easy to obtain.

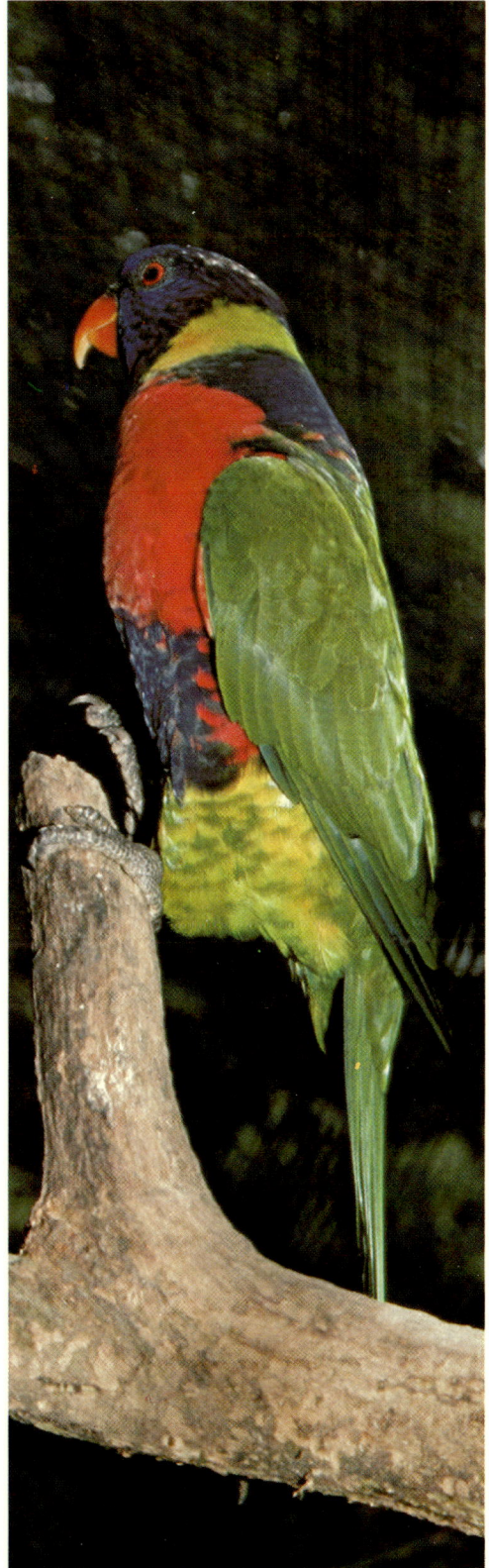

Tree limbs make the best perches. This is the subspecies *moluccanus* of the Rainbow Lory, *Trichoglossus haematodus*.

Perching in the aviary should be functional and easy to clean. As a general rule it should be at or just above head height, to give the birds confidence. Most of it should be horizontal, although there should always be one reaching from the floor up to the shelter where the food is placed. It is also useful to have a perch within jumping distance of the entrance to the nest box as the cock will often perch there on guard while the hen is on eggs. The main parts of the perching should be divided between the front and the back of the aviary, with plenty of clear flying space in between the two.

Perch sizes should vary slightly so that the birds' feet do not suffer from cramp. The perching should be replaced if most of the bark has been chewed off, as this is the birds' sole source of chewing material in order to keep the bill and claws at the right length.

Finally, the last consideration when building the aviary is to include wherever possible a shallow bathing area for the birds. Lories and lorikeets have some of

The aviaries at Birdworld are arranged so that the public may view the birds from one end of the flight space.

the brightest and glossiest plumage of all birds and enjoy bathing and preening themselves regularly. This water, as with any other water offered to the birds, should be changed daily, and if possible it should be situated under a covered area of the aviary to minimize any possible risk of contamination from the excretion of native birds perching on or flying over the aviary.

Pest Control

The two main sources of contamination of an aviary by pest species is either from excretion through the roof by birds walking on top of an aviary or flying above, or from small birds or rodents finding their way into an aviary and contaminating the food and water of the captive birds.

Any such contamination of the aviary is highly dangerous to captive birds inside because their health is more vulnerable from the stress of being imported, being subjected to weather and climates different from those they may be used to, possibly being underweight or over, and possibly being weakened as they become used to a diet different from what they have been fed on before. All these considerations lead the captive birds to be more susceptible to common avian diseases, such as avian tuberculosis which can be carried harmlessly by native birds but can have dangerous results on captive stock. The possibility of problems are dramatically reduced if the captive birds have been bred in captivity, but all psittacines are among the most susceptible of birds to diseases.

The first source, contamination entering the aviary by excretion, is not a major problem as long as the food of the captive bird is sheltered and the water, if in a dish, is also sheltered or the bathing area, if one is present, is cleaned daily.

If perches in the aviary are installed above eye level, the birds will feel more secure. These are Little Lorikeets, *Glossopsitta pusilla*.

The second source is the more common cause of problems. With larger lories it is tempting to use a larger size of wire: although this may well keep the lories in, it may well permit small birds or mice to squeeze in and gain access to the food supply. If the wire is a suitable size and there are no gaps around the door, then mice may still gain access through the floor of the aviary. Ideally the base should be concreted, but if this is not viable then the floor of the aviary can be covered with wire and a level of sand or gravel an be used to cover this.

As a final point, if food is being taken to a large number of aviaries, steps should be taken to ensure that the food is not contaminated before it reaches the aviaries. Having worked in bird gardens, I am familiar with whole communities of native birds which seem to live by waiting for the keeper to enter an aviary and then flying down and feeding from the dishes remaining on the food trolley. To prevent this, any food left unattended should be well covered against the attention of native opportunists.

Aviaries Used at Birdworld

At Birdworld, a large number of pairs of similar lories and lorikeets are housed in a row, so it was necessary to consider what steps could be taken to improve hygiene and reduce any risk of disease being spread through the collection. The diagram shows a side section of an aviary showing the concrete floor being sloped into a drain. Over the top of this is a layer of strong mesh, then a layer of large stones. At least three times a week, unless the birds are breeding, any pieces of chewed perching are removed from these stones, which are then washed with a high-pressure hose, as is the brickwork. The birds soon become used to this routine and simply fly into the shelter, where the door can be shut until cleaning is finished. The food and water are placed inside the shelter to prevent contamination. The shelters and the doors to the aviaries open only to a heated corridor, which not only provides heat but also contains birds should any fly out while the door is open. The front sections of wire on the aviaries can also be removed to assist in the refurbishment of aviaries. These aviaries work well, with the only noticeable thing lacking being bathing areas; this is under review. In the meanwhile, the birds do enjoy regular light spraying from a hose in summer during the mornings of warm days, and also have a large water dish inside the shelter.

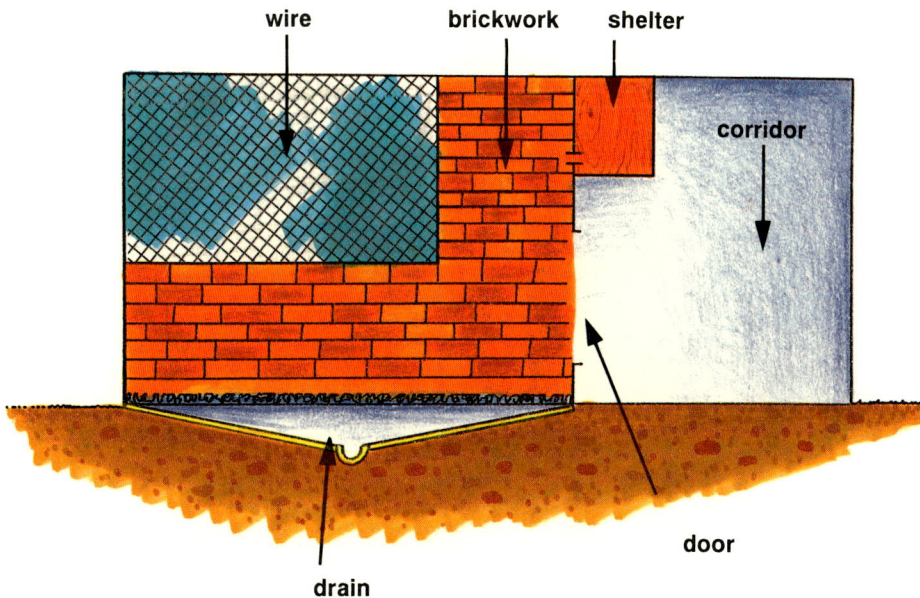

The lory aviaries at Birdworld incorporate a heated shelter as well as a flight area with a wire floor for ease in cleaning.

Yellow-and-green Lorikeets, *Trichoglossus flavoviridis*. Food is offered in an earthenware bowl designed to facilitate perching on the rim.

Diet

Lories and Lorikeets are widely known as brush-tongued parrots. This is because of the elongated papillae which are present on the tongue and act as a type of brush that assists the bird while feeding on pollen or nectar. It is therefore assumed that the diet of these birds in the wild is predominantly a mixture of pollen and nectar. This assumption however would be flawed, as many species of Loriinae inhabit areas where such supplies of nectar or pollen are only available seasonally, and birds in such areas even breed and rear young when nectar is not available. It must also be remembered that species in the group Loriinae vary widely, with some smaller species, such as *Neopsittacus*, being highly reliant on small seeds in their diet, while the larger *Chalcopsitta* species take virtually no seeds. The presence of a brush tongue in Loriinae parrots should therefore be considered as an adaptation to help them make use of an available food source, in this case, nectar and pollen. It does not mean that in the wild the birds will not take other foods; indeed, both in the wild and in captivity fruit and vegetable matter is an important part of the diet of these birds.

There are also field records of these birds eating aphids and other such opportune foods as may be available. It would be wrong then in captivity to feed all Loriinae species the same basic nectar mix without searching for other foods to supplement their diet.

In captivity, in the past as well as the present, they thrive on a wide selection of artificial nectar mixtures with some fruit also being added. Many people new to aviculture avoid this group of birds because they believe them to be difficult to feed and because they think they are too time consuming to look after. While it is true that in warm weather the nectar mixture will need to be replaced more than once a day to prevent it from going off, even so, lories and lorikeets are not hard to look after. Modern artificial diets take a minimum of preparation, some only needing warm water to be added. Thus lories are no more time consuming than any other group of parrotlike birds. Indeed, the differences between the lories and other psittacines are not as marked as many people believe.

In recent years there has also been an artificial dry food devel-

Pollen and nectar are important elements in the natural Loriinae diet. This is the Scaly-breasted Lorikeet, *Trichoglossus chlorolepidotus*.

oped, which, although not yet widely used, shows considerable promise. Currently, various problems are surfacing, but it remains hopeful that these will be addressed in time, so that dry foods can confidently be used to facilitate lory keeping.

Artificial Nectar Diets

Various forms of artificial nectar diet have been used successfully for several decades in aviculture and are by far the most basic diets used with captive lories and lorikeets around the world. The exact contents of the diet vary widely but are normally made up from a mixture of the following ingredients: baby-milk powder, baby-food mixtures, honey, sugar and warm water. Condensed milk

and natural yogurt are also widely used, but they tend to go off quickly in warm weather. These home-made recipes are nowadays being replaced by a wide selection of artificial-nectar-mix products which usually require that only warm water be added.

An absorbent food item such as sponge cake or bread can be added to the nectar, which will soak up the mixture and allow the birds to eat it without lapping. There should always be an excess of liquid available, though, for any birds which prefer to drink. Such a medium in the nectar will also provide roughage in the diet, which is badly lacking in many captive-lory diets. Fruit should also be available to the birds either in the main mixture or hung separately in the aviary on available perches. The type of fruit used should be varied to assist the diet, but sweet fruits such as pawpaw, banana, peaches, and kiwi fruit are taken with most relish.

If you are making up your own nectar mix it is important if you are using a recipe that contains either sugar or honey to make sure that, as a general rule, the mixture is too thin rather than too thick. Both sugar and honey if given in too generous quantities can cause digestive problems and can also cause problems with fungal infections of the mouth and throat. If the mixture is too thin then the only consequence will be that the birds will have to eat more and the food dish should be checked more regularly; but if on the other hand the diet is too thick and too rich, then the birds could well suffer from long-term liver and kidney problems.

As briefly stated earlier, any artificial nectar mix, particularly if it contains honey or sugar, will be prone to going off during periods of warm weather. For this reason, in summer the mixture should be renewed at least twice a day, especially if breeding is taking place. In winter as well the mixture should be renewed at least twice a day, and the birds will greatly appreciate this warm diet during periods of cold weather. As a final point, it should be remembered that artificial nectars tend to be sticky and sweet and are a perfect possible source of bacterial disease. For this reason, the food containers should be cleaned out at every feed, thoroughly, to prevent any such problems.

Dry Diets

The recently available dry diet is in a powdered form which is liberally sprinkled over segments of fruit or is mixed in with chopped fruit. I have not used this diet extensively myself but from conversations with Keith Mitchell, formerly head keeper of the Leeds Castle Aviaries, I learn that there the diet has been used successfully for several seasons, with breeding taking place with birds fed on the diet, with few problems. One observation made was that the droppings of birds fed on this diet were much more solid than usual. One slight disadvantage was the birds' habit of placing the powder in their bathing area, which had to be checked and refreshed frequently.

Fruit and Supplements

Fruit offered to the birds should vary, but as already mentioned sweet fruits such as banana, pawpaw, and kiwi fruit are taken with most relish. When these are out of season, however, a wide selection of fruits will be taken,

A group of *Eos* and *Trichoglossus* lories gather on the feeding station, which contains a fruit mixture.

Here lories are feeding on a nectar mixture offered in stainless-steel trays.

from pears, apple, strawberries, plums, and grapes, as well as many others. Artificial nectar products which just require adding water usually have most of the added vitamins and minerals needed, and even home-made recipes are normally sufficient if they contain baby-food products. Indeed, adding many multivitamin products can be counterproductive, as the slightest taste of bitterness in the food can put them off feeding for the day. Calcium in the form of cuttlefish bone may be hung in the aviary and a product such as Collo-Cal-D, which is normally given to bitches weaning puppies, can be added to the mixture with no hindrance to the birds' appetite.

Seeds, although fed widely in the past, need not be given to most lories and lorikeets, although small amounts of sprouting seeds (excepting sunflower) may be beneficial to some wild-caught birds which are not feeding well. Some seed should, however, be given to smaller lorikeet species such as the Iris Lorikeet (Trichoglossus iris). Some species, such as the Emerald Lorikeet (Neopsittacus pullicauda), are quite dependent on it. As a general rule the feeding of seed is discouraged for the larger species, as there are many reports of young chicks in the nest box dying as a result of being fed almost exclusively on seeds by the parent birds. Such larger species should instead receive more fruit and vegetable matter in their diets.

Diets at Birdworld

When first experimenting with the lory diet here at Birdworld, we erred on the side of caution by making the diet slightly too dilute. It soon became apparent however from the amount of food the birds were consuming that the diet needed to be slightly stronger. We use Milupa baby food in addition to a manufactured nectar mix to increase the protein level slightly to that nearer to the level of pollen, which is the wild food of most species. We also found that Zoo-A pellets, when placed in the mixture, were rather too absorbent, so we soak them overnight before adding them to the mixture. A keen eye is kept to see to the individual preferences of different birds, and the amount is varied accordingly.

The main morning diet is listed below, and a reduced feed of 200ml instead of 250ml is given without fruit and other additives as an evening feed and in summer also at midday.

Morning Feed: Each pair of birds receives approximately 250ml of nectar, which is made up of the following: 35ml of Birdquest International Nectar diet; 15ml of Milupa baby food; 200ml of warm water.

To this basic diet is added the following for each pair: one pre-soaked SDS Zoo-A pellet; a small amount of boiled rice; diced apple or pear; two out of the following fruits: grapes, kiwi fruit, banana, plums, strawberries, peach, pawpaw.

For these Red Lories, *Eos bornea*, apple and orange have been impaled on the perches.

A Yellow-streaked Lory, *Chalcopsitta sintillata*. A lory of this size is properly restrained by controlling the head with one hand and supporting the body with the other.

Health Care

This chapter is included to give the novice some guidelines as to the routine health care of lories and lorikeets in his care. It also lists some of the more common illnesses which may afflict birds. It is however beyond the scope of this book to give detailed information as to the varying treatments of these diseases, as this is a job of a vet. Once a serious problem is diagnosed in a bird, home remedies are highly discouraged unless undertaken by a very experienced bird keeper. The first section on handling and restraint is included as safe and confident handling of birds is important for such routines as moving, worming and the trimming of claws and mandibles where necessary.

Handling and Restraint

Larger lories such as those of the genus *Chalcopsitta* have powerful bills and can inflict painful bites. For this reasons as well as reducing stress to the bird, handling should be kept to a strict minimum.

In the capture and moving of birds direct handling is not necessary, providing suitable equipment is used. A proper catch net should have enough depth to it that a bird can, once in the back of the net, be held there simply by turning the net so that the bird's weight against the net rim prevents escape. Once secured in this manner the bird can then be transferred to a suitable carrying box by placing the opening of the net against the opened door of the box and allowing the bird to walk in. The carrying box should be dark but well ventilated to reduce stress. It should have a central perch in it, on which the bird can sit fully upright without banging its head on the roof, and of course it should be strong enough to stand up to damage from the bird's bill, if the bird is to be kept in there for a number of hours.

There are occasions however when it will be necessary to physically handle the bird. These occasions could include worming and trimming of the bill or claws. In the case of a bird that looks ill in an aviary, it is advisable to capture the bird to examine it for any obvious signs of ill health, such as a blocked vent or seeing if the bird is underweight by feeling how much fat there is covering the rib case. If this is the case, then light leather gloves can be worn to give extra confidence, but when wearing gloves an even closer eye must be kept to ensure that the grip

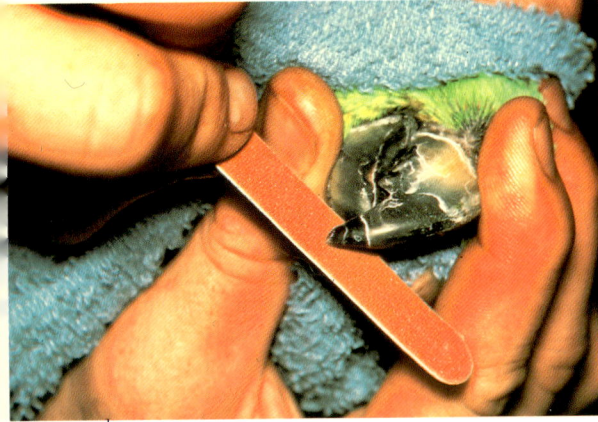

An emery board or similar tool can be used to return the bill to its natural shape.

around the bird's neck and windpipe is not too tight. If the bird is in an aviary, it should first be contained by capturing it in a net. Once captured the entrance of the net should be held against the wire side of the aviary with a slight opening at the top. The bird should then attempt to climb up the wire and will grip it with its bill. Once its bill is holding the wire, then a hand can grasp the bird around the sides of the head with the thumb and forefinger, meeting under the bird's lower mandible. This grip should be secure but it should also allow the bird to move its head slightly from side to side but not up and down. In the case of a larger lory, the second hand should immediately secure the remainder of the body so that the bird's struggling does not lead it to injure itself. Once secured, the bird, if still holding the wire, will usually release it quite easily, and whatever needs to be done to the bird can be achieved with the assistance of a second person.

Trimming the Bill and Claws

The reason why a bird's bill or claws become too long is usually because there is insufficient chewing material present in its enclosure. Perching should be replaced regularly, and in the case of a newly received bird that has an overgrown mandible, plenty of soft wood will often reduce this problem without actual trimming of the bill being necessary.

If claws need to be trimmed then only the tip should be removed. It should be remembered that if the claws are allowed to grow long, then the length of the vein inside also grows; so that long claws cannot be cut right back to their normal length without causing bleeding. Therefore only the tip should be removed and the rest left to improved perching and general management.

If the bill is to be trimmed, then this should be done with care so that the shape of the bill remains the same. Also, care should be taken to protect the bird's tongue which will almost certainly try to probe what is going on. As with the claws, only a small amount should be removed and the rest left to the bird itself with improved chewing material available.

If problems persist and the bird is unable to assist itself even with appropriate chewing material available, then it is best to seek the aid of a veterinary surgeon. This can also be done in the first case if the keeper is not confident about the procedure or if there is no one available to help.

Feather Care

When lories and lorikeets are in good health, their plumage is always in good condition, being bright and shiny. Problems can and do arise from time to time. These can be the result of bad management, poor health, behavioral problems, parasites or disease. As part of their care lories and lorikeets should wherever possible have access to bathing water. In summer they bathe frequently and spend much time afterwards preening themselves in order to keep their feathers in prime condition. If it is not possible to provide a bathing area, then the birds should receive regular light spraying with lukewarm water. Problems can occur, particularly in summer, with birds that are kept inside, and the atmosphere can become too hot and dry. The feathers can start to look ragged and to lose their oil through overpreening, as the birds feel uncomfortable. The simple solution to this is increased ventilation and more frequent spraying. If the birds are only in quarantine or waiting to go outside, then the problem should disappear when they do go outside.

Occasionally and again more often with birds kept inside, problems can occur with new feathers growing through and not losing the protective sheath. Normally this is removed by the bird but if the bird is feeling unwell or if the air is very dry the sheath can become dried out and stick to the feather. If this happens it is quite a simple job to gently run the thumb nail down it against the index finger. This should form a seam and the sheath can easily be removed. This is most common in wing and tail feathers but can also be a problem on the heads of pets and hand-reared birds who have no companion to preen this area for them.

Feather plucking is most commonly a problem in pet birds which are kept on their own. It can affect birds to different extents but in at least three cases I have seen the bird has been completely lacking in feathers except for the head, which the bill can not reach. Many different reasons can account for this

Growing feathers are enclosed in a protective sheath, which becomes brittle and is removed by preening.

With appropriate preventive measures, feather lice such as these of the order Mallophaga should not be a problem.

behavior, but the most common is a mixture of boredom and frustration at not being able to attract the attention the bird craves. Hand-reared pet birds, particularly members of those species which in the wild occur in flocks, are completely dependent on the owner to provide the companionship and artificial preening behavior that the bird craves. The most obvious answer to this problem is to spend as much time as possible with the bird; where this is not possible, occupational alternatives such as more and differing chewing material should be provided.

Very occasionally a problem can arise in a pair of birds, with one partner plucking the other. If this proves too much of a problem, then there is little alternative to separating them and trying to pair them to different birds. Likewise, if a problem occurs with parent birds plucking a chick in the

latter stages of its period in the nest box or just after it fledges, there is little alternative but to remove the chick and finish rearing it by hand. This, if it happens, is a behavioral fault in the parents and is likely to reoccur. If the chick is left with the parents, long-term damage can be done, especially in the development of the wing feathers, so it is best to remove all chicks from such parents.

Feather problems from disease or parasites are rare, especially if captive-bred stock is always bought in preference to wild-caught birds. Certain problems can crop up, though. Mites can afflict captive birds, but suitable dusting powders can be obtained from a vet. Much more of a problem is a thankfully rare virus which appears after two or three molts in captivity, nearly always in stock which has been wild-caught. The effects of the virus are to progressively make the feathers more brittle, until the bird losses the ability to fly and is eventually devoid of nearly all feathers. Although the bird can survive for a number of years, no effective treatment of this viral condition has yet been found.

Worming

Worming in adult birds should be carried out at least twice a year as a matter of routine. In addition, it is also good practice to worm young birds after they leave the nest box. Regular worming of adult birds should be undertaken because, although they may be long-term captives, there is a constant risk to aviary birds of infection from wild birds whose excretion may fall into the aviary. There may be an even greater risk if small native birds can gain access to the aviary in order to feed from the food dish. Fledgling birds should be wormed on becoming independent, as the nest box can become extremely fouled during rearing, even if the substrate is changed more than once. Such environments are perfect breeding grounds for parasites, and the young could even be infected directly from the parents during feeding.

A wide selection of different worming products are available, but at Birdworld we dilute Panacur 10% solution by half so that a 5% solution is given at 0.4ml per kilogram of the bird's body weight. Usually the bird will accept a blunt instrument which is placed into the mouth to keep it slightly open while the wormer is introduced slowly at the back of the throat, taking care that it avoids the respiratory tract. The bird will usually lap and swallow slowly. In the case of a stubborn bird that will continually reject this, the wormer can be given directly into the crop but this should be done with the assistance of an experienced bird keeper or a vet.

Common Worms

Roundworm, the most common worm encountered, is usually fairly harmless to most birds, only using them as an intermediate host. If the worms are present in large numbers, however, they could weaken the health of the host bird and open the way for other opportunistic infections to develop.

Tapeworm segments in the small intestine. Routine worming will keep such parasites in check.

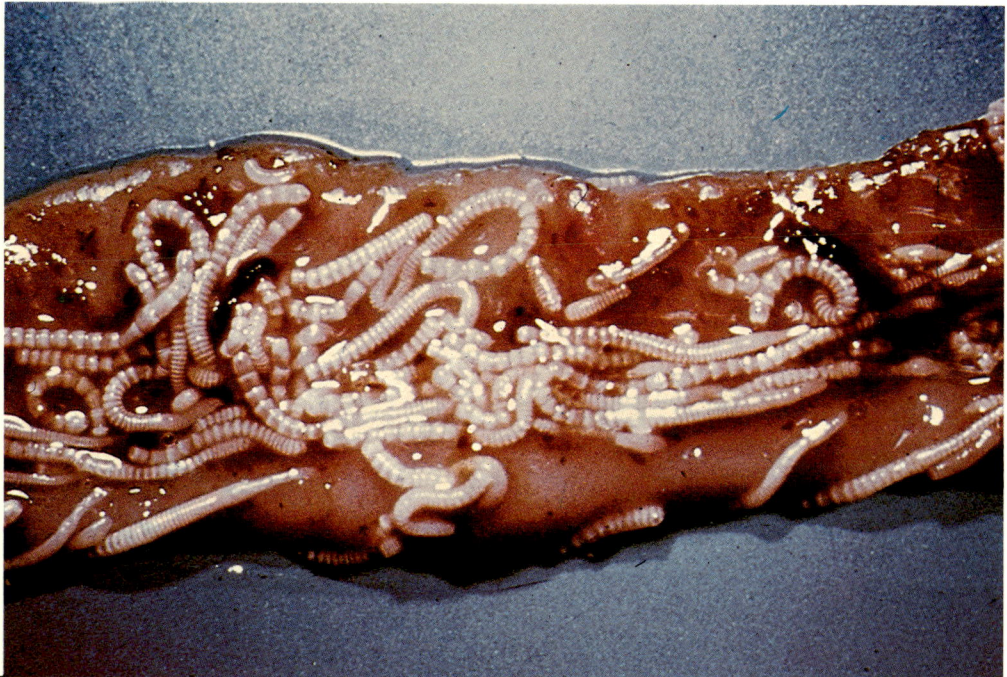

Ascarids are closely related to roundworms and are frequently found in psittacines. These larger worms can clearly be spotted in the bird's excretion and should be dealt with quickly, as they can cause a blockage of the small intestines, leading to possible paralysis and even death of the bird.

Tapeworms require an intermediate host, so they are unlikely to cause problems except if they are present in newly imported birds.

Care of Ailing Birds

The signs of ill health in a bird can vary from having a "fluffed-up" appearance, having the eyes partially closed, being unsteady on its feet, having a poor body stance with its wings drooped and having very labored and weak flight. If an aviary bird shows any or all of these indications, then it should be caught up and examined for obvious problems such as injuries, parasites or having the vent blocked. If there is no obvious reason for its poor condition and if there is not enough fat covering the breast bone as would be ideal, then it would be wise to move the bird inside to a heated room. Often the cause might be simple, such as the bird being slightly bullied by its partner and not receiving enough food, or just a delicate bird feeling chilled after a cold night. It is always better to err on the side of caution, though; in such cases, pull the bird inside

Some incidence of parasite infestation is typical in wild lory populations (such as the *Trichoglossus* flock seen here).

to a warm cage. The importance of heat in such cases cannot be overemphasized, as it can often be the difference between the bird living or dying.

In extreme cases were the bird is very weak, the use of an hospital cage would be of great benefit. It should have a controllable heat source situated below the bird. It should be well ventilated, have a single perch low to the floor, and heating. It should be able to be covered to reduce stress and disturbance to the bird. If very weak the bird should receive small but regular feedings by hand of liquid food. This will be accepted better if it is warm. This care should be continued until a veterinary surgeon can be contacted or until the bird is strong enough to feed itself.

Cuts and Infections

Recently imported birds which have been wild caught should be closely inspected for any lumps in the body plumage, which may conceal a cut or other injury which has turned necrotic. Should such a lump be found, then it should be dealt with quickly by a veterinary surgeon. Cuts and infections are rare in established birds unless they result from fighting. However, the undersides of the feet should be inspected from time to time as splits in the skin can lead to infections such as bumblefoot.

Eye Injuries

It is quite common in newly imported birds which have been kept in large numbers in a con-

Lories housed in outdoor aviaries (this is a Yellow-streaked, *Chalcopsitta sintillata*) must be watched carefully for signs of illness.

fined space to have minor eye infections, and even grazing or bruising of the eye. Infections can usually be spotted as the bird will keep the eye partially or completely closed, with often some swelling present to the upper and lower eyelids. Grazing and bruising can normally be seen on close inspection. All of these problems can easily be dealt with by using the relevant eye drops or antibiotics from a vet.

A healthy looking Red Lory, *Eos bornea*.

Psittacosis

Psittacosis, or parrot fever as it is commonly known, is perhaps the best known of all avian diseases. This is probably due to the fact that it can be passed on from the bird to its keeper, often with serious results. Psittacosis is a viral infection, and often strong birds can carry it with little effect. Indeed, many native birds, particularly pigeons, are known to carry the virus.

It is probable that birds in the wild state can carry the virus with little effect, but when subjected to the stress of capture and transportation with the resulting poor health, they can then succumb to the virus. It is also likely that

birds arriving in poor health after importation are prone in their weakened state to possible infection from native birds. However, psittacosis is in fact quite rare in captive lories.

It is in parrot species that the virus is best known, possibly because of the close contact between owner and pet bird. This close contact may allow the virus to be passed either in water droplets or dust. Signs that the bird has psittacosis start with general signs of ill health, bad body posture, listlessness and droopiness. This is followed by diarrhea, nasal discharge, disturbance to the breathing, lack of appetite and deterioration of health, leading to death. Once the virus has taken hold, there is little hope for recovery, and those birds that do may serve to infect others.

Respiratory Infections

Fungal infections of the respiratory tract can sometimes be common in birds which have been subjected to importation in large numbers. Aspergillosis is the most common. It is an opportunistic infection that may occur in a bird that has been stressed, particularly if in confinement with others.

The main signs are rapid and labored breathing. Often, disturbance to the respiratory tract by loose patches of fungus can be detected on close listening.

Throat and Crop Infections

Fungal infection of the throat and crop, most commonly candidiasis, can be found in imported birds mostly for the same reasons as those for respiratory infections: overcrowding, stress and general poor health.

The main signs of the infections are poor health. The bird will often move its head and bill in an uncomfortable manner, and sometimes patches of dead fungus can be seen in the back of the throat. Labored breathing, loose droppings and regurgitation may also occur.

Avian Tuberculosis

This bacterial infection can often be carried by birds in the wild as well as in captivity for a number of years without any noticeable effect on them, until it is triggered of by periods of poor health or sudden stress. It is also possible that captive-bred birds can be infected from contact with native birds.

Signs of the disease are those of general poor health, and often a bird will appear slightly unwell one day and be found dead the next with no obvious reason on first inspection.

Salmonellosis

This highly infectious disease can originate from a bird new to the collection carrying it, but most often it is the result of contamination of the birds' food supply by native birds or rodents. The worst offenders include mice, sparrows and robins.

Signs of the disease are general poor health, loss of appetite, shivering, rapid breathing and off-colored droppings, sometimes containing blood. The condition usually deteriorates, leading to death.

Beak-and-Feather Syndrome

Thankfully, this condition is still rare and has not been widely reported in the Loriinae. This condition starts to appear in newly imported birds after the second or third molt in captivity. New feathers that come through are brittle and break easily. Such feathers cannot stand up to preening, and so eventually the bird is left virtually featherless and flightless. The beak also then becomes soft and grows too long, requiring frequent trimming. The cause of the condition is now known to be a virus, and work is underway to find a treatment.

Papuan Lorikeets, *Charmosyna papou.*

Cardinal Lories, *Chalcopsitta cardinalis*. Leg ringing (banding) remains the most practical method of identifying individuals.

Breeding

Once a suitable true pair of birds are established in an aviary, then it should not be too long before an attempt at breeding is made. As already said, most lories and lorikeets will prove willing breeders if they are in good condition and have a suitable nest site provided for them, either in an aviary or in an inside breeding cage.

Management of Breeding Birds

If a long-term breeding program is to be attempted, especially with one of the rarer species when getting fresh blood may prove difficult, then it is important to be able to keep track of individual birds and blood lines. Many young parrotlike species nowadays are close rung while in the nest box or during hand-rearing, yet there are still many people who don't like this, the most common argument being that the ring could become tangled with the aviary wire or a perch and cause the death of the bird. This has sadly happened in the past, although it is extremely rare. One only has to look at such examples as the keeping of birds of prey, where the close ringing of captive-bred birds has been compulsory for several years, to see that

problems with rings, even when used in large numbers, are comparatively negligible. The presence of a ring can also be of use if, as is often the case, a surgically sexed pair of birds is obtained and one subsequently dies. It is then necessary to either have a post mortem on the dead bird carried out or have the remaining bird re-sexed in order to ascertain the correct sex of the remaining bird.

Close-rung rings all have an individual number which can be used to keep check on the bird, but as an extra step a simple record card can be filled out for each young bird bred, which not only may prove of future help to you but also to anyone who may later purchase birds from you.

The record card might include such data as: Species; Date of hatching; Ring number of the bird; Male parent's ring number; Female parent's ring number; Number of young in clutch; Whom bought from; and Whom sold to.

If birds are to be kept on a colony basis, then the use of colored rings will enable the keeper to keep check of which birds pair up and breed together and so prevent accidents where the wrong bird is removed from the colony. Two rings should be used for each bird. The first ring should be either red or blue to show that the bird is either female or male respectively. The second ring should be a different color, such as orange, green, white, black, purple or pink. Each of these colors can be used only once in each gender although a male and female may have the same second color as they can be differentiated by the color of their first, sex ring. Using this simple system, up to six pairs of birds may be kept together but still be monitored and a check kept as to the parentage of any resulting chicks.

Once a pair do start to nest, then they do not require too much assistance but rather privacy. Observations should be made from a distance. If it is a pair's first attempt at breeding and once the first egg is laid, I would rec-

ommend that the nest box is not checked again until the eggs are due to hatch, unless there is something in the birds' behavior to indicate that all is not well and the eggs may have been damaged or abandoned.

Depending on different views, nest boxes should either be checked quickly but regularly or left alone while the birds are incubating. Most parent birds will become used to being checked quickly every couple of days, but in the case of a first breeding attempt it is probably better to leave them well alone. The best time to check the nest box is while food is being given to the birds. This is the one time in the day when the birds are expecting you to enter the aviary, and they will be distracted slightly by the presence of food. Entry into the aviary at any other time will be

Courtship feeding between a pair of Rainbow Lories *Trichoglossus haematodus haematodus* atop their nesting log.

seen by the birds as a direct threat.

Food should always be available and should be replaced frequently during hot weather. The presence of fruit segments is especially important at this time. Depending on the diet already being given, it may be beneficial to add other items such as egg biscuit, dried egg, skimmed dry milk, and baby food such as Farex while chicks are being reared. At Birdworld all these items are added to the set diet of lories rearing young, with quantities of 25mg of each item being given to breeding birds in every feeding.

Once the chicks are two or three weeks old it may be necessary to clean the interior of the nest box, which can become extremely fouled as chicks are growing and so can become infested by maggots if not checked regularly. If it is necessary to change the substrate, then, after the box is replaced on the wall, a close eye should be kept to ensure that the parents return to brood the chicks as normal. When it is time for the chicks to leave the nest box, most lories will accept this periodic cleaning of their nest box, but extra care should be taken if it is a new or particularly nervous pair of birds that are nesting.

When it is time for the chicks to leave the nest box, then it must be checked to be sure that they can do so. Badly built nest boxes without a ladder up to the hole can lead to chicks not being able to exit and lead to death, once the parents stop feeding them. It is for

A Duyvenbode's Lory, *Chalcopsitta duivenbodei*, perched in an aviary, with the shelter visible in the background.

this reason that many people prefer slightly sloped nest boxes, which help chicks climb to the entrance.

Once the chicks are outside the nest box, the parents should continue to feed them for a number of days. However, until a chick can fly well and knows its way around, an extra food dish should be placed on the floor of the aviary to ensure that the chick can wean itself without too much trouble finding food. If the chicks are the result of an early spring clutch of eggs, care must also be taken that they do not fall victims

In mixed collections, interspecific bonding can occur. The billing here is between a Rainbow Lory *Trichoglossus haematodus rubritorquis* and a Meyer's Lorikeet, *Trichoglossus flavoviridis meyeri.*

they should be about the same length and width as the birds' body length and should be about three times deeper in height. Standard nest boxes at Birdworld used for lories and lorikeets are 28cm by 28cm by 80cm in height. The entrance-hole size is important as it will affect how confident and safe the hen feels while nesting. It should ideally be slightly larger than the bird, but the bird should be able to block it completely while sitting in it to prevent intruders entering. If standard nest boxes are brought in, the the size of the hole can be altered by tacking on strips of wood over two sides of the hole to make the entrance a more suitable size. The box should be hung against a secure wall or beam of the aviary that does not allow too much movement of the box. Installing various types of boxes and at somewhat varying heights about in the aviary will give reluctant-to-breed pairs a maximal variety of nesting sites to choose among. The top of the box should be removable for servicing, and it should ideally also have an inspection hatch on the side for quick inspections of the eggs or chicks. A perch should be present on the front of the box, or very close to it, to allow the cock bird to perch there on guard while the hen is brooding inside; later, it will help the young birds in fledging.

to a sudden hard frost. If one is predicted, then it is usually a safe precaution to replace the chicks in the nest box at dusk where they will probably roost until the next morning. There should also be plenty of perching around the nest box so that young fledglings can return to the box on their own if they want to.

Another safe precaution at this stage is to worm the chicks which may have become infested, as a result of being fed by infested parents, during their time in the nest box. Such infestations can considerably weaken the health of a young bird that is still developing, and may even lead to death.

Nest Boxes

The exact sizes of nest boxes can vary, but as a general rule

Standard lory nest box used at Birdworld, with the inspection hatch visible on the side.

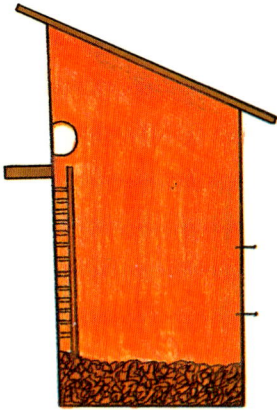

Standard and sloping nestbox designs, showing the nesting substrate and the position of the internal ladder. Such a ladder serves to prevent damage to the eggs by the parent birds, and it later helps the youngsters to fledge.

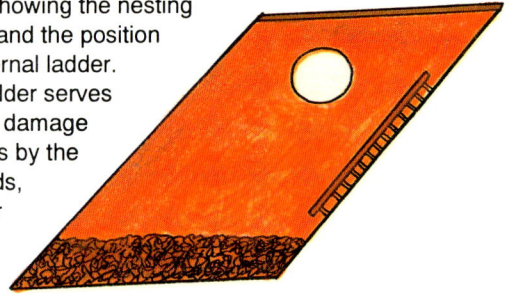

A recently hatched Scaly-breasted Lorikeet, *Trichoglossus chlorolepidotus*, is mostly naked except for the sparse down feathers.

Some people worried about chicks climbing out of the nest box are now using sloping nest boxes, which have been widely used for breeding softbilled birds. These seem to work well, but are usually unnecessary if a standard-shaped box is equipped with an adequate ladder up the front side, leading to the entrance hole. Such a ladder can usually be made of wire mesh secured over two strips of wood.

Nowadays L-shaped nesting boxes are being used increasingly. These boxes offer the advantage that a parent bird rapidly entering the nest box when disturbed will not land on top of its mate or the eggs, as these are positioned away from the entrance hole. Also, the bend also makes the nest space more secluded, darker, and more secure.

Whatever kind of box is used will need to be replaced from time to time, but any new box should of course be identical to the old one, if the birds have already bred in it. If the birds have not yet bred, then it is better to have one of each box type present in the aviary and to let the birds choose for themselves.

An adult Violet-naped Lory, *Eos squamata*, with its two recently fledged youngsters.

The type of substrate that should be used is also the subject of great debate. I now use wood chippings exclusively and have had fcw problems. I have also used a mixture of peat and sawdust in equal parts. Some people dislike using peat as if very dry it can be dusty, but I find that if peat is not used the medium is too loose and the scrape excavated by the birds is likely to cave in on top of the eggs. Sand and shingle are also used by some aviculturists.

The depth of the substrate should be about 10cm to allow the birds to make a scrape in which to lay. The stated substrate is reasonably absorbent, but if allowed to become too foul it can prove an ideal home for maggots and parasitic worms in hot weather. It may then be necessary to replace it, particularly in the case of species, such as the Blue-streaked *(Eos reticulata)*, which may spend up to twelve weeks in the nest box before fledging. In addition, small drainage holes can be bored in the bottom of the box; this helps to lessen the problem of fouling.

Pieces of soft wood should also be attached to the interior of the nest box, on the sides. This will provide chewing material for the adult birds, which will help prevent boredom and will also provide a means of venting any frustration away from the chicks which are being reared. The resulting chewed wood will also provide fresh bedding to go on top of the fouled bedding as the chicks develop.

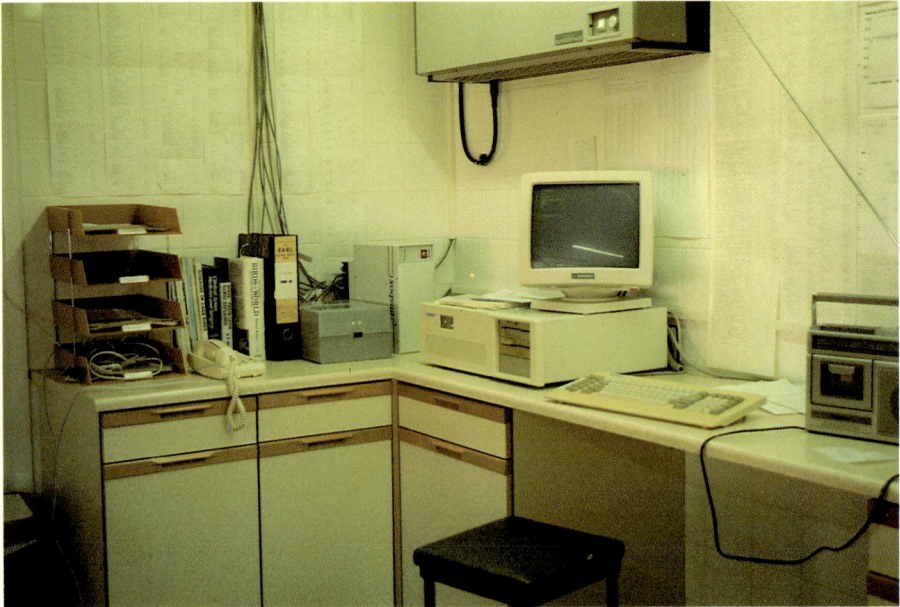

Two views of the incubation room at Birdworld. The computer is used to track egg development, producing graphs to summarize each egg's progress.

Artificial Incubation

In certain cases, where a particular pair of birds prove unreliable as parents or in the case of the sudden death of one or other of the parent birds, it may be necessary to remove the eggs and incubate them by another method. The practice of artificial incubation has increased dramatically over the course of the last decade, especially in the case of psittacines. As many of the rarer species begin to breed in captivity, it is now standard practice to remove the first and often second clutches of eggs to be hand-reared and then to leave the adult birds to rear the last clutch of eggs themselves. This allows for the maximum number of birds to be produced from the limited number of adults in captivity. At the same time, it still means that the adults are allowed to rear young themselves every year, which is important if they are not to become disenchanted with attempts to breed. The same practice is also used with common parrots, with the first two clutches being removed to be hand-reared as pets, while the later, parent-reared birds are usually held back or sold as future breeding stock. In the Loriinae, which are widely known for their habit of breeding through the winter months, any such eggs are often removed, as at

Goldie's Lorikeet, *Trichoglossus goldiei*, at thirty-four days of age.

such times of the year the chicks are frequently lost through chilling when, after about ten to fourteen days, the parents start to leave them for longer periods of time between broodings. As a general rule, though, it should not be necessary to remove lories for hand-rearing unless the parents prove unreliable, as most captive lories are prolific breeders anyway, often rearing at least two clutches a year on their own without any artificial help apart from extra food being offered.

Fostering Eggs

If it happens that you have a pair of birds which normally produce infertile eggs and are sitting at the time when you need to remove eggs from another pair of birds for some reason, then the option of using the first pair of birds as foster parents can be considered. Fostering is best tried only during the summer months, as in winter the foster parents, like the normal parents, can leave the chicks for longer periods after the first couple of weeks, leading to chilling.

If fostering is to be attempted, then two important considerations should be taken into account.

A nestling Black Lory, *Chalcopsitta atra*.

Firstly, the size of the egg in comparison with that which the foster parents would normally lay must be considered. Most lory and lorikeet eggs are of a similar size, but if the difference is too great, then this could lead to the eggs not being brooded or turned correctly. The second consideration is the length of the incubation time and how long the prospective foster parents have been sitting. If the foster parents have already been sitting their own eggs for a number of days and then are given fresh eggs to sit, then they are unlikely to sit these new eggs for a further full term. Many psittacines will break their eggs once they have sat them full term with no sign of hatching, and this could well prove the case if they are expected to sit for too long.

It is worth remembering however that the first fourteen days of incubation are the most delicate, so it may be worth giving the eggs to foster parents for this period and then finishing off incubation in an incubator. This could well be worth considering if the keeper has not had extensive experience of incubators. Finally, it should not be forgotten that when the eggs are changed over, the eggs originally belonging to the foster parents should always be candled to ensure that they are indeed infertile. Candling and examining the size of any air sac present can also give a good indication as to how old the eggs are if this is not otherwise known, and so help indicate how long the foster parents have already been sitting.

A Yellow-and-green Lorikeet, *Trichoglossus flavoviridis*, almost at fledging age.

Incubation Using Broodies

The types of birds normally associated with the practice of brooding eggs of different species are chickens, most commonly bantams. However, because of the small size of lory and lorikeet eggs, using even the smallest breeds of bantam is impractical. Some success has been achieved though using domestic pigeons. This method however is dependent on having a reasonably large number of pigeons available because their own incubation time is usually shorter than that of most Loriinae species, and it is probable that the pigeons have already been sitting their eggs for several days. It is necessary then to remove the eggs at around half term and place them under a pair of pigeons that have only just completed their clutch in order to ensure that they are not abandoned.

The main disadvantage to this method is that domestic pigeons can carry several diseases which can be spread to psittacines. These cannot be transmitted through the shell but can be transmitted from pip onwards. Care should therefore be taken that eggs are always removed in advance of pipping. Also, care should be taken that if broody pigeons are allowed to fly outdoors, then their excretion is not allowed to contaminate aviaries occupied by psittacines.

The Incubator

The type or manufacturer of the incubator that is to be used is not really of any great importance, although a moving-air incubator that is equipped with a fan and automatic egg-turning trays is naturally going to be more accurate and easier to use than a more old-fashioned, still-air type of incubator. The needs of an egg, if it is to develop properly during its incubation period, are that it must first be subject to a suitably constant temperature, usually in the region of 37.4° C, with little or no variation. Most modern, commercially manufactured incubators are equipped with very accurate thermometers which work well. But when first setting up a new incubator, two or three accurate thermometers should be placed in different areas of the incubator so that any significant variation can be noted. All thermometers can be subject to varying every so often, and for this reason, every six months some of the existing thermometers that have been in use should be returned to the manufacturer to be calibrated against a factory standard to ensure that they are still giving an accurate reading. Many people now use electronic thermometers which, while proving more reliable and easier to read, do however have the disadvantage that they can be subject to quite significant initial calibration errors. However, as long as the differential is known and taken into account, then there should be no problem, and such thermometers normally go on to prove to be highly reliable.

The next important requirement if an egg is to develop properly is that the atmosphere within the incubator is such that it holds a constant level of humidity in the incubator air supply that can be varied according to the needs of an individual egg. The reason why humidity is important to a developing egg is that as the embryo within the egg develops, a steady rate of water evaporation takes place from the egg into the atmo-

Thirty-six-day-old Perfect Lorikeets, *Trichoglossus euteles.*

Two nestlings of the yellow-backed subspecies of the Chattering Lory, *Lorius garrulus flavopalliatus*.

sphere to allow a suitable-sized air sac to develop within the egg shell, which will prove essential to the developing chick immediately prior to hatching.

The most conventional method of measuring humidity is by using a hygrometer, but this has proved to be highly inaccurate when the fine measurements used in egg incubation are being attempted. Instead, incubator manufacturers have found a much more accurate instrument that can be used to keep track of the level of humidity within an incubator: the wet-bulb thermometer. The wet-bulb thermometer works in exactly the same way as a normal thermometer does, except for the fact that the end is covered by a wick made up of many stands of light cotton. This is connected to a water supply which soaks up through the wick and evaporates from around the thermometer bulb. This leads the thermometer to give a lower-than-normal reading, as the evaporation of moisture from the wick has a cooling effect similar to that which can be felt by moistening a finger and holding it up in the wind. The exact level of this cooling effect is dependent on three main factors: temperature, air circulation, and air humidity. In an incubator the temperature and rate of air circulation are always constant, which means that the only variable factor which will affect the reading of the wet-bulb thermometer is the level of humidity. It is necessary, however, to regularly check the wicks to ensure that they receive a constant supply of water and that they are not becoming contaminated by a build-up of calcium and other residue that may be left by the evaporating water. To further this point, as most of the water used by an incubator is for evaporation purposes, it is important that only distilled water is used at all times, to avoid problems from any build-up of residue caused by impurities in the water.

The third main necessity for an egg to develop properly is the need for a correct type and amount of turning in order to simulate the actions of the hen bird sitting on and brooding the eggs. During natural brooding egg turning is done in a very random fashion, so it is important when simulating this in an incubator that the egg is turned in alternating directions. If an egg is turned continually in the same direction, then this will lead to one of the suspensory ligament coils becoming wound up, with the opposite one becoming unwound, leading to the yolk becoming loosened and causing

Blue-crowned Lory chick, *Vini australis*.

Rainbow Lories, *Trichoglossus haematodus*.

the death of the developing embryo. When artificially turning eggs, it is best to turn them through 180° at least five times a day. Eggs can be marked on opposite sides of their shells with X and O symbols in order to make it simpler to tell at a glance whether each egg has been turned in conjunction with the others. Many incubators use tilting trays which hold the egg in an upright position and then tilt to 45° in each direction alternatively in order to turn the eggs. While this method has proved successful in the large-scale incubation of poultry eggs, there are doubts when this method is used with parrot eggs, which have a much smaller yolk, in comparison to the albumen. This can lead to incomplete growth, with not all the available space inside the egg being utilized if eggs are not also turned by hand through 180° over the pointed axis of the egg.

It should of course be remembered, when opening an incubator to turn eggs, that this should be done as quickly as is safely possible and that the heating and humidity controls should be turned off immediately prior to opening. Once the incubator has been shut and the heating is turned back on, the humidity should not be switched on again until the incubator has returned to its normal temperature in order to prevent fluctuations in the level of incubator-air humidity.

Given the correct maintenance of these three main factors, a fertile egg should successfully develop, no matter which type or manufacturer of incubator is used to house it.

Ornate Lory, *Trichoglossus ornatus*.

Development of the Egg

Although the main method of tracking a fertile egg's development is to measure the rate of water loss from the egg, progress can also be seen by "candling" the egg. "Candling" is a term used to describe the use of a directed light source that can be used to shine light into the interior of an egg so that its stage of development can be visually monitored. This is a valuable aid to successful incubation, not only enabling any abnormalities or embryo deaths to be seen before they are otherwise detectable but also allowing the keeper to gain a much better understanding of what is happening during incubation.

The time periods between candlings should be at least forty-eight hours to ensure that the eggs are not unduly disturbed too often. In the regular routine of the author, eggs are weighed on one day and candled on the following day, with both weighings and candling taking place at forty-eight hour intervals. Each egg is different, as speed and patterns can vary between different eggs, but the following signs should be apparent with candling:

Day 5: The egg should show clear signs of fertility as a small red circle with a thin line visible in the center.

Day 10: Growth should now be clearly visible from a pattern of veins usually concentrated down one side of the egg.

Day 15: Growth should be extensive, completely surrounding the air sac and reaching down towards the point of the egg.

Day 20: Growth should by now be covering all of the available space within the egg, although this may spring back from the point a couple of days before hatching.

Day 24: The chick within the egg should be approaching internal pip, if it has not already broken through into the air sac. The shadow of its bill pushing against the membrane may be seen. If this is visible, turning of the egg should stop, and the egg can be moved to the hatcher when the membrane has been broken.

If for any reason the developing embryo has died during incuba-

tion, this can usually first be seen by the veins starting to break down, and the red lines, which are usually quite sharp, become blurred and unclear.

Weight-loss Management of Eggs

During incubation an egg should lose a set amount of weight, due to water loss between the time it is laid and the time of the internal pip. Weight loss is never measured until the time of hatching, because once the shell has become pierced at the start of hatching, water loss will suddenly become extremely rapid and will cause confusion if trying to calculate an overall weight loss.

The ideal weight loss for a lory or lorikeet egg is in the region of 14–15%, although any weight loss which falls in between the general

A group of Newlife 75 incubators in use in the incubation room at Birdworld.

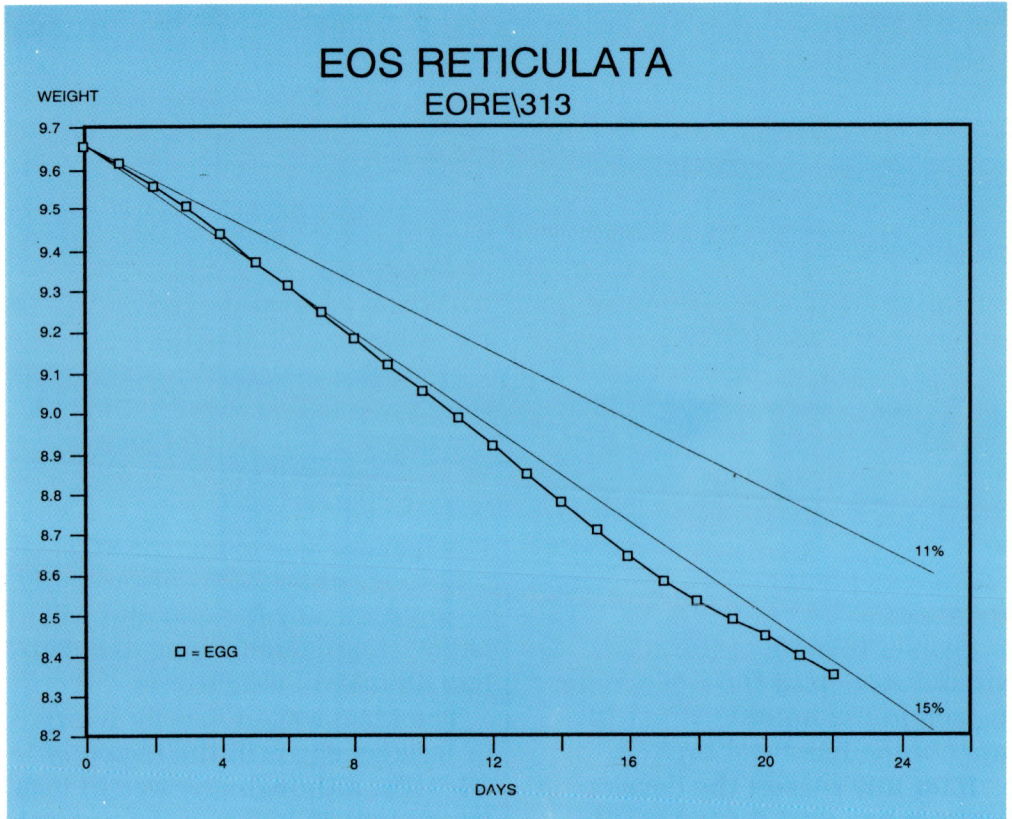

Weight-loss graph of a Blue-streaked Lory egg.

avian guidelines of 11–15% should result in a successful hatch. The effects of incorrect air humidity in the incubator during incubation can be fatal. If the incubator is kept too dry, then weight loss can be too rapid, leading to a much enlarged air sac and a shrinkage of the egg's contents. This in turn leads to small, feeble chicks which cannot fully utilize calcium for bone growth and have underdeveloped kidneys which fail to function properly. Such chicks, if they survive incubation, almost certainly die during hatching. Alternatively, if the humidity of the incubator is too high, this can lead to not enough weight being lost, which leads to a small air sac and the presence of unused amounts of albumen. Such chicks are often soft and flabby and need to hatch prematurely because of the lack of sufficient air in the much-reduced air sac. The exact needs of different eggs can vary greatly, though not only because of species but also because of the diet of the adult birds, how many eggs have already been laid by the hen, and even the genetic combination of the parents affecting the porosity of the egg shell. It is necessary then, particularly through the first ten to fourteen days of incubation, which are the most important, to individually monitor the progress of weight loss for each egg and alter the humidity accordingly to produce a successful hatch.

If a number of eggs are being incubated at the same time, then it will not be possible to alter the humidity in the incubator because of one egg, as this may adversely affect the development of the other eggs. The easiest method then for controlling the humidity level for a number of eggs is to set up a group of independent incubators, each with a different humidity level. Normally, three incubators are used to start with: one set at zero humidity, one set at average humidity of around 81° F (28° C) on the wet-bulb thermometer, and the third incubator being as humid as can be easily achieved. Setting up an incubator at zero humidity can be difficult unless it can be set up in a room with a dry atmosphere, as there is little point doing it in a room where the air is humid. At Birdworld the incubation room is equipped with a dehumidifier so that the level of humidity in any of the incubators can range from near zero to nearly 100%.

When measuring the weight of an egg it is important to keep the time periods between the weighings constant, otherwise the results of the weight-loss graph will become misleading. Some people weigh eggs daily, but I have found that weighing every second day is just as accurate and less disturbing to the running of the incubator. The weights can then be plotted onto a graph. This graph uses egg-density measurements, but it is to all intents and purposes the same as a weight-loss graph, with the 11–15% lines marked as a guide. It can be seen from the weight-loss graph that the egg was running just below the 15% line. With its placement into a maximum-humidity incubator after its arrival at a hand-

Chicks of the subspecies *forsteni* of the Rainbow Lory, *Trichoglossus haematodus*, already exhibit the basic areas of adult coloration.

Blue-streaked Lory, *Eos reticulata*.

rearing agency, the weight loss reduced to a near-perfect 14% at the time of hatching.

If you do not have time to compile weight-loss charts for each egg, then some idea of their progress can be gained simply by using the following equation:

Freshly laid egg weight multiplied by the desired percentage of weight loss to pipping, divided by the number of days to pipping.

The result of this equation is the daily amount of weight that should be lost by the egg if it is to reach its desired weight loss by the time of internal pipping. If the measurements acquired from weighing the egg vary greatly from the daily weight-loss figure given by the equation, then a more detailed graph will have to be prepared in order to ascertain the problem with the level of weight loss and then to correct the rate of water loss from the egg.

Egg Density

Egg density is really just an extension of measuring weight loss, but instead of measuring the reducing weight against the egg's original weight, egg density measures the reducing weight against a calculation of the egg's volume, which helps standardize eggs of different sizes and initial weights so that they can be more easily compared. As an example of this, two eggs from the same species can vary in their initial weight, and so cannot easily be measured against each other on the same graph. But even though their sizes and weights differ, because they are the same shape and consist of

The Newlife 75 incubator is a moving-air unit that will maintain a stable humidity level.

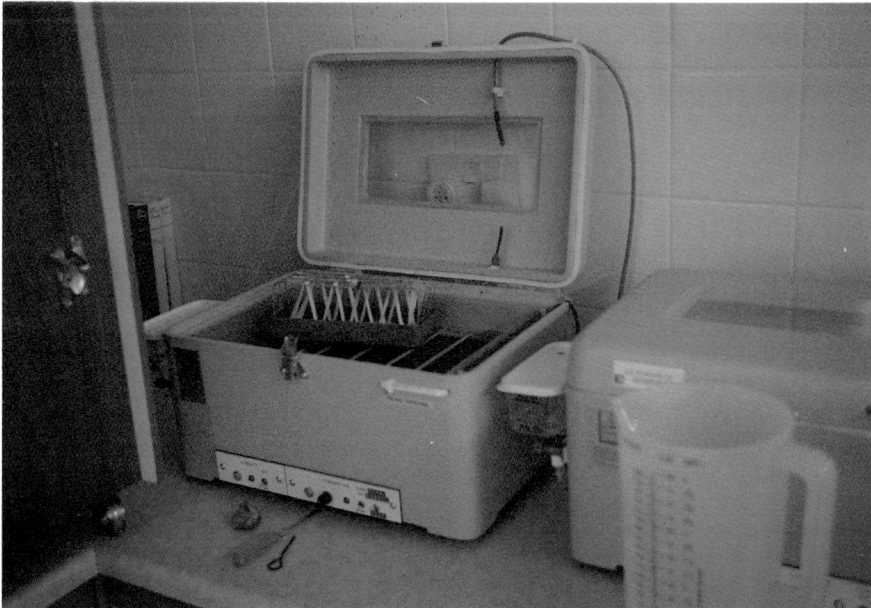

the same substances, by calculating their volume they can be brought much closer together. Volume is calculated by measuring the egg's length and multiplying this against the breadth squared, and finally against a constant figure of 0.51, which allows for the egg's shape:

Egg volume equals length multiplied by breadth, again multiplied by breadth, multiplied by 0.51.

This measurement of volume can then be divided by the weights of each weighing to show the level of reduction in the egg's density. With most psittacines, the reduction should be a constant 0.006 daily:

Egg density equals egg volume divided by egg weight.

For general incubation, though, there is no need to use egg density unless you intend to compare the incubation of large numbers of eggs at a later date. Measuring weight loss normally is just as accurate and requires much less time than using egg-density measurements.

Hatching

The time for an egg to be removed from the incubator and placed into the hatcher is straight after the chick has broken through the membrane between itself and the air sac. The differences between the hatcher and the incubator are firstly that the eggs are not turned in the hatchers; secondly, the level of humidity in the hatcher is always kept high to prevent problems from

chicks drying out rapidly once they have hatched; and, thirdly, the hatcher is normally run at a slightly lower temperature than the incubator because towards the end of the period of incubation the chick that is hatching is fully formed and generating some body heat of its own, which may lead to it overheating in the high humidity if the hatcher ran at 37.4° C as in the incubator; thus 36.5° is the normal temperature for the hatcher. Hatching can be a slow process, and it is therefore useful for the hatcher to have a viewing panel; otherwise, the temptation is strong to keep opening the hatcher to check the progress of the chick. Such temptation should be strongly resisted, as each time the hatcher is opened, the level of humidity that is necessary inside the hatcher is lost. If this happens too frequently as the chick is trying to hatch, it can leave the chick dehydrated and considerably weakened.

Helping the chick to hatch is a dangerous exercise and should not be attempted by anyone without experience unless the chick is excessively late in hatching and appears weakened. Small segments of the shell can very slowly be loosened from the egg, but at the first sign of blood the chick should be left alone, as this is a sign that the chick is not yet ready to hatch. On hatching, the chick should be left in the hatcher to dry out for around four to five hours before being moved to a brooder.

Young Rainbow Lory still in the nest box. This is the subspecies *Trichoglossus haematodus capistratus*.

Incubation Times

Listed below are the known incubation times of many species of lories and lorikeets.

Black Lory: 25 Days
Black-capped Lory: 25 days
Black-winged Lory: 26 days
Blue-streaked Lory: 26 days
Cardinal Lory: 24 days
Chattering Lory: 26 days
Dusky Lory: 24 days
Duyvenbode's Lory: 24 days
Fairy Lorikeet: 25 days
Goldie's Lorikeet: 24 days
Iris Lorikeet: 23 days
Josephine's Lorikeet: 25 days
Little Lorikeet: 23 days
Meyer's Lorikeet: 23 days
Mount Apo Lorikeet: 23 days
Musk Lorikeet: 25 days
Musschenbroek's Lorikeet: 25 days

Ornate Lorikeet: 26 days
Perfect Lorikeet: 23 days
Purple-bellied Lory: 26 days
Purple-capped Lory: 26 days
Purple-crowned Lorikeet: 22 days
Rainbow Lorikeets: 23–26 days
Red Lory: 24 days
Red-flanked Lorikeet: 25 days
Red-spotted Lorikeet: 23 days
Scaly-breasted Lorikeet: 23 days
Solitary Lory: 30 days
Stella's Lorikeet: 26 days
Striated Lorikeet: 25 days
Tahiti Blue Lory: 25 days
Ultramarine Lory: 25 days
Varied Lorikeet: 22 days
Violet-naped Lory: 26 days
Wilhelmina's Lorikeet: 23 days
Yellow-and-green Lorikeet: 23 days
Yellow-bibbed Lory: 25 days
Yellow-streaked Lory: 26 days

A young Chattering Lory *Lorius garrulus flavopalliatus*.

Hand-Rearing

On hatching, the chick should be allowed to dry for about four to five hours before being removed to a brooder, where it can be given a small initial feed. In the case of chicks which have had a prolonged and difficult hatch, some warm water containing glucose can be given even earlier. Many authors state that no food should be given for any reason up to forty-eight hours, but I find this is unnecessary and may well lead to dehydration in a weakened chick.

Brooders

The type of brooder used does not matter, whether it is a converted incubator or a home-made one, as long as it is well ventilated and able to hold a steady temperature without fluctuation; is easy to clean and sterilize; and has enough space to incorporate a container to hold the chick for the first few weeks while it is unsteady in its balance. If a converted incubator is to be used, care must be taken that there are no exposed wires which the chick may reach and chew.

The chick should be placed into a container slightly larger than itself which is waterproof and easy to clean. Old margarine tubs often serve this purpose well. The floor and sides should be covered with absorbent paper towels. The texture of the floor should be slightly uneven, to help in the development of the feet by giving them some thing to grip against. If the chick is housed on its own, then the sides should be padded so that the chick, which is very unsteady to begin with, can lean against the padding to help it maintain an upright position. This is particularly important just after it has been fed.

Hygiene should be strict, especially in the first few weeks. The paper in the container should be changed at every feed, and the interior of the brooder should be cleaned with a sterile wipe daily.

Temperature

On its removal from the hatcher, the chick should be placed into a brooder of similar temperature, around 36.5° C. This temperature is slowly reduced while the chick is being reared— just under a degree a day, so that by the time the brooder reaches room temperature then the chick should be well feathered. However, it should be remembered that each chick is an individual, and a temperature which will suit one chick may well prove uncomfortable to a chick of similar age and species. Temperature changes should therefore depend on the chick's reactions to them as well as its age.

If a chick is too cold then it will lose its pinkish color and feel cold to the touch; it may well even shiver. Being too cold can lead to problems in digesting food already present in the crop and can open the way for opportunistic diseases and infections which can quickly kill a weakened chick.

Signs that the chick is too warm are that it will be lethargic and feel hot to the touch. The chick will not feed and will regurgitate food that has already been eaten. The exact temperature at which the chick is to be kept, then, depends on the chick itself and whether it is comfortable and feeding well.

Humidity is not critically important during the rearing period, with normal room humidity being quite adequate in the latter stages of rearing. However, some care should be taken in the early stages to ensure that the chick is not allowed to become to dehydrated at the higher temperatures at the start of the rearing period. It is therefore advisable to place a small, shallow container of water, covered by wire, into the brooder in the early days of the chick's life.

Diet and Feeding

A multitude of different diets can and have been used in the hand-rearing of lories and lorikeets. If you use a diet with success, then there is little reason to change it. I now use a hand-rearing diet called Avi-Plus, to

A corner of the incubation room at Birdworld. After hatching, the chicks are removed to another room for hand-rearing.

Hand-reared chicks of the Blue-streaked Lory, *Eos reticulata*, aged forty-two days.

which I add a small amount of a commercial nectar mix called Lory Nectar.

A simple diet that will be successful can be made of baby foods: 2 parts of cereal and 1 part mixed fruits, brought to the desired consistency with a little nectar. Most baby-food products, in whichever combination they are used, have all the added vitamins and minerals needed for the healthy growth of the chick. Additional vitamins and minerals are not therefore needed and, if used, should be used in moderation.

The two main reasons for dietary problems during hand-rearing are firstly due to a higher level of protein in the diet which usually leads to the death of the chick; this can be countered by using a lower-protein diet if problems are encountered.

The second most common problem is that of the crop becoming impacted. This is usually caused by the food mixture being too thick, but can also be caused by a drop in the chick's body temperature while digesting a feed or by an infection of the crop. The food mixture should therefore

WEIGHT GAIN OF TWO EOS RETICULATA

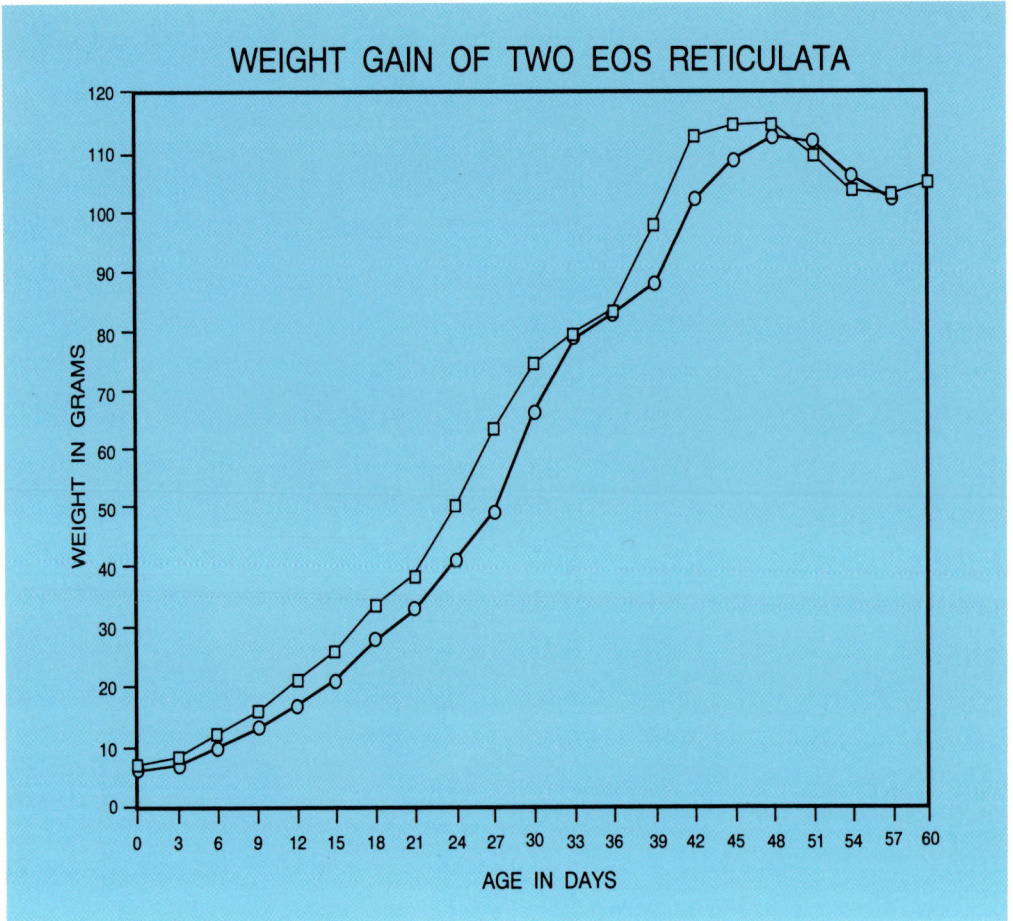

Comparison of the weight gain of two Blue-streaked Lories during hand-rearing.

always be fed too dilute, in preference to being too thick. Food that is too dilute has no harmful effects other than that the food is digested more quickly and more frequent feeding is required. On the other hand, food that is too thick can cause crop impactions and other problems.

Times of feeds are normally every two hours from 6 A.M. through to 12 P.M. to begin with. In the case of a weak chick that has had a prolonged hatch, an extra feed at 3 A.M. is advisable for the first few days. As the chick grows, the food mixture can become thicker and, as this will take longer to digest, the chick can take more food at each feed. The time periods between feeds can be lengthened. This is normally done by omitting one feed at a time and readjusting the time periods accordingly. As a general rule, the chick should be ready for its next feed about twenty minutes after the crop has completely emptied from the previous one. When adjusting the feeding times, a watch should also be kept on the chick's weight-gain chart to ensure that it is still growing at a correct rate.

Before feeding the chick, the feeding utensils as well as the food should be warmed up to the chick's body temperature and kept warm during feeding. This is easily done by warming the food gently in a microwave and warming the feeding utensils by placing them in hot water. The food dish can then also be rested in a larger container of hot water to help it maintain its temperature during feeding, if more than one chick is to be fed.

There are two main types of feeding utensils that are used: a syringe or a teaspoon with the sides bent up to mimic the lower mandible of the adult bird. I prefer the latter, for as well as stimulating the bird to feed with its bill in a more correct position, using the spoon allows the bird more control over the speed at which it accepts food without being forced.

When feeding the chick, first the tissue it is housed on should be changed and examined to ensure the chick is excreting properly. Then the vent should be checked to ensure that it is clear and not blocked. Most importantly, the crop should be checked to ensure that it is completely empty after its last feed. If even the tiniest amount of food is left, never be tempted to top this up but rather return the chick back into its brooder and try to

feed again after about half an hour, by which time the crop should have cleared.

If the crop will not clear within a reasonable time period, then it may be impacted and no more food should be given until this has been cleared. The first step should be to give the bird some warm, slightly saline water, and as this is taken, very gently massage the crop area. With luck, this will help dissolve any blockage. But if this fails, the immediate assistance of a vet will be required, otherwise the chick is likely to die. If the problem lies in the chick not excreting normally and the vent is not blocked, then the lower abdomen and area around the vent should be gently massaged with a cotton-wool bud.

Some of the implements that have proved useful in hand-rearing parrot chicks.

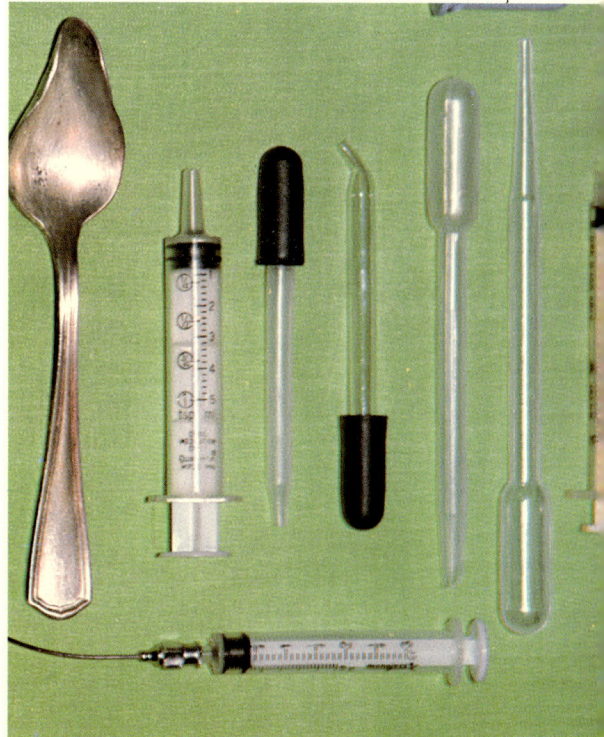

if this yields no result, then a small, blunt metal instrument can be gently warmed and carefully placed into the entrance of the vent and slowly moved from side to side. This should stimulate the chick to pass waste, just as the cleaning motion of the parent bird does in the nest. If everything is all right, then the chick can be fed by supporting its body in the correct position and allowing it to feed from the spoon, which the chick will soon learn to do quite aggressively. Care must be taken that the crop is not over filled; during the day, filling it to two-thirds capacity is quite adequate. If the skin looks stretched and shiny, then the crop is too full. As well as possibly leading to impaction or damage to the crop, over-feeding can lead to a young chick not being able to support itself properly and becoming stuck or even choking.

Once the chick has received enough food, then the bill and body should carefully be cleaned to remove any excess food or excretion that may be present on the chick. Separate tissues should be used for the cleaning the bill, the body and the vent. The chick should then be placed back into its container on fresh tissue and put back into the brooder, taking care that it is in a comfortable

Dusky Lory, *Pseudeos fuscata*, at thirty-seven days of age.

Nearly seven weeks old, these Yellow-and-green Lorikeets, *Trichoglossus flavoviridis*, are fully feathered but paler versions of the adult birds.

position and can support itself without too much effort.

As the chick grows and becomes steadier, it should be allowed more room for movement. After about fourteen days, the chick if possible should have slight differences in temperature within its brooder, allowing it to either lean into or away from the heat and so start to regulate its own temperature. It is also important to check that the feet are developing properly: if confined and gaining weight too quickly, the feet and legs can become malformed. If in doubt, it is a good precaution to place sterilized twigs in the bottom of the container, which will provide exercise for the feet.

Ages at which different species of lories and lorikeets become independent vary, but the long process of weaning can usually start from the sixth week onwards. This is easier in the Loriinae than in other parrots, as the adult food of these birds is also in liquid form. The diet should therefore slowly be changed to that of the adult birds, and the dish of food can be left with the chick between feeds so that the chick can start to feed itself. The chick will soon get the right idea but to begin with will need regular cleaning as it experiments with taking food from a dish. Segments of fruit may also be given for the chick to experiment with.

The sole member of the genus *Pseudeos*, the Dusky Lory, *P. fuscata*.

Species of Loriinae

The standard for the classification of Loriinae species was set out by Joseph M. Forshaw in the classic book *Parrots of the World* in 1973. Forshaw recognized eleven genera and fifty-five species of lories and lorikeets, as shown below.

Chalcopsitta
Black Lory, *Chalcopsitta atra*
Duyvenbode's Lory, *Chalcopsitta duivenbodei*
Yellow-streaked Lory, *Chalcopsitta sintillata*
Cardinal Lory, *Chalcopsitta cardinalis*

Eos
Red Lory, *Eos bornea*
Black-winged Lory, *Eos cyanogenia*
Blue-streaked Lory, *Eos reticulata*
Violet-naped (Violet-necked) Lory, *Eos squamata*
Red-and-blue Lory, *Eos histrio*
Blue-eared Lory, *Eos semilarvata*

Pseudeos
Dusky Lory, *Pseudeos fuscata*

Lorius
Chattering Lory, *Lorius garrulus*
Black-capped Lory, *Lorius lory*
Purple-capped (Purple-naped) Lory, *Lorius domicellus*

Purple-bellied Lory, *Lorius hypoinochrous*
Yellow-bibbed Lory, *Lorius chlorocercus*
White-naped Lory, *Lorius albidinuchus*
Stresemann's Lory, *Lorius amabilis*
Blue-thighed Lory, *Lorius tibialis*

Vini
Blue-crowned Lory, *Vini australis*
Kuhl's Lory, *Vini kuhlii*
Stephen's Lory, *Vini stepheni*
Ultramarine Lory, *Vini ultramarina*
Tahiti Blue (Tahitian) Lory, *Vini peruviana*

Phigys
Solitary (Collared) Lory, *Phigys solitarius*

Trichoglossus
Rainbow Lorikeet, *Trichoglossus haematodus*
Ornate Lorikeet, *Trichoglossus ornatus*
Cherry-collared (Ponapé) Lorikeet, *Trichoglossus rubiginosus*
Perfect Lorikeet, *Trichoglossus euteles*
Scaly-breasted Lorikeet, *Trichoglossus chlorolepidotus*
Yellow-and-green Lorikeet, *Trichoglossus flavoviridis*

The Black Lory, *Chalcopsitta atra*, is a large species that adapts well to aviary life and is disposed to breed under proper conditions.

Iris Lorikeet, *Trichoglossus iris*
Varied Lorikeet, *Trichoglossus versicolor*
Goldie's Lorikeet, *Trichoglossus goldiei*

Glossopsitta
Musk Lorikeet, *Glossopsitta concinna*
Purple-crowned Lorikeet, *Glossopsitta porphyrocephala*
Little Lorikeet, *Glossopsitta pusilla*

Charmosyna
Papuan Lorikeet, *Charmosyna papou*
Josephine's Lorikeet, *Charmosyna josefinae*
Red-flanked Lorikeet, *Charmosyna placentis*
Striated Lorikeet, *Charmosyna multistriata*
Wilhelmina's Lorikeet, *Charmosyna wilhelminae*
Fairy Lorikeet, *Charmosyna pulchella*
Palm Lorikeet, *Charmosyna palmarum*
Meek's Lorikeet, *Charmosyna meeki*
Red-chinned Lorikeet, *Charmosyna rubrigularis*
Red-throated Lorikeet, *Charmosyna amabilis*
Red-spotted Lorikeet, *Charmosyna rubronotata*
Duchess Lorikeet, *Charmosyna margarethae*
Blue-fronted Lorikeet, *Charmosyna toxopei*
New Caledonian Lorikeet, *Charmosyna diadema*

Oreopsittacus
Arfak Alpine (Whiskered) Lorikeet, *Oreopsittacus arfaki*

Neopsittacus
Musschenbroek's Lorikeet, *Neopsittacus musschenbroekii*
Emerald Lorikeet, *Neopsittacus pullicauda*

While this book follows the above classification set out by Forshaw (1973), three of the above species are left out of the descriptions, as they are either no longer considered distinct species or are extinct. These are as follows:

Stresemann's Lory, *Lorius*

amabilis, is known from only one specimen, and no further birds have ever been recorded. The species is almost identical to *Lorius hypoinochrous,* the Purple-bellied Lory, but lacks any black coloring. Forshaw suggests that the type specimen might be a specimen of *L. hypoinochrous* in which the gene controlling the black pigmentation had mutated, and this lack of black coloring can account for all the distinctive features of *L. amabilis.* As no further birds have been recorded, this is the most likely explanation.

The Blue-thighed Lory, *Lorius tibialis,* is again only known from one specimen examined in 1867. There is some dispute, but in the absence of any further birds being recorded it is now regarded as a variant of the Purple-naped Lory, *Lorius domicellus.*

The New Caledonian Lorikeet, *Charmosyna diadema,* is recognized as a distinct species, but no specimens have been captured since 1860. There are some unconfirmed sighting recorded in the 1950s, but as these cannot be confirmed and because of the time period involved since the last capture of specimens, it is unfortunately almost certain that this species is extinct.

Description of Birds

In this book the description of bird topography is standardized by using the sections of the body illustrated and named in the drawings of the bird's body and wing anatomy following. The length of a bird is given as a measurement from its bill to the tip of the tail feathers—this is usual but not always the case in other books. All details of length, color and other distinguishing features are given in the descriptions as those of the nominate subspecies, or race, then variants from this in other subspecies are given afterwards.

The confiding nature of many lories has increased the appreciation of them as tame companions. This is a Rainbow Lorikeet, *Trichoglossus haematodus.*

Topography of the Wing

1 - Primaries; 2- Secondaries; 3 - Bend of Wing; 4 - Alula; 5 - Primary Coverts;
6 - Lesser Wing Coverts; 7 - Median Wing Coverts; 8 - Secondary Coverts; 9
- Tertials; 10 - Lesser Under Wing Coverts; 11 - Greater Under Wing Coverts;
12 - Axillaries.

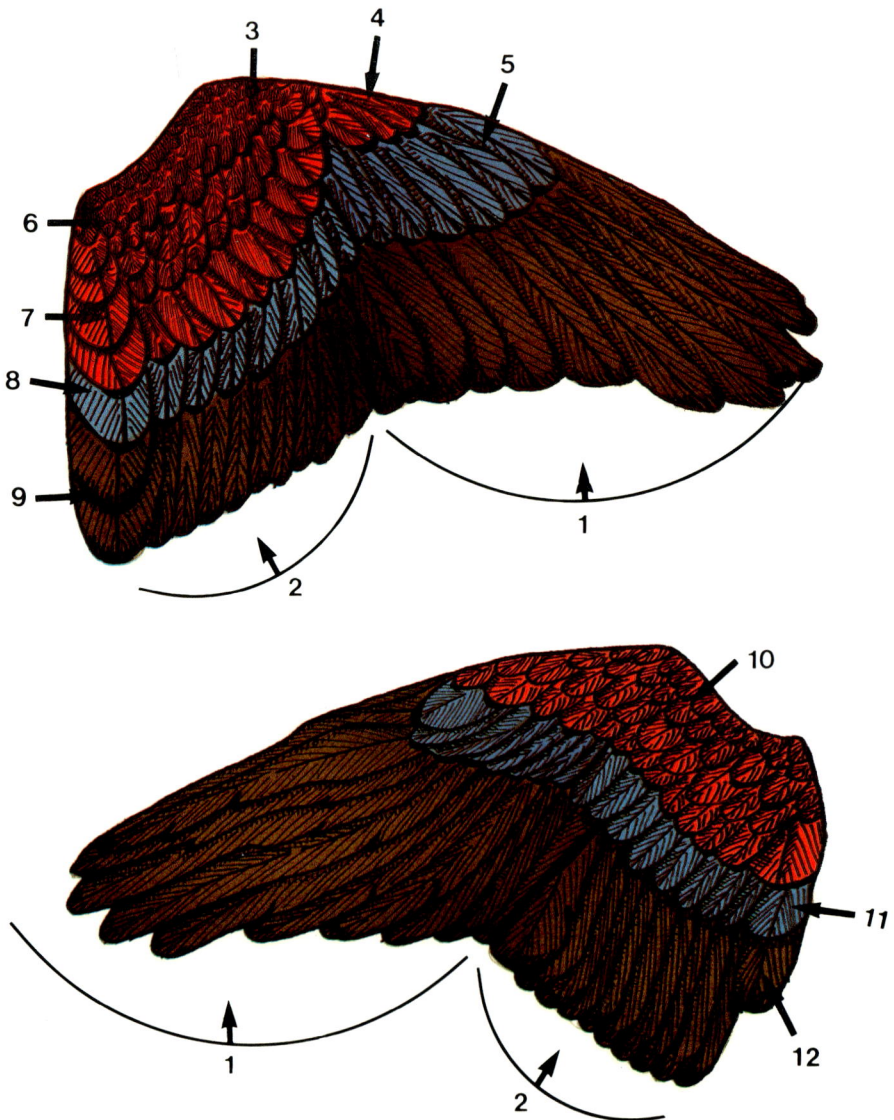

Topography of a Lory

1 - Crown; 2 - Nape; 3 - Ear Coverts; 4 - Mantle; 5 - Back; 6 - Rump; 7 - Central Tail Feathers; 8 - Lateral Tail Feathers; 9 - Thighs; 10 - Abdomen; 11 - Breast; 12 - Throat; 13 -Lower Mandible; 14 - Upper Mandible; 15 - Cere; 16 - Lores.

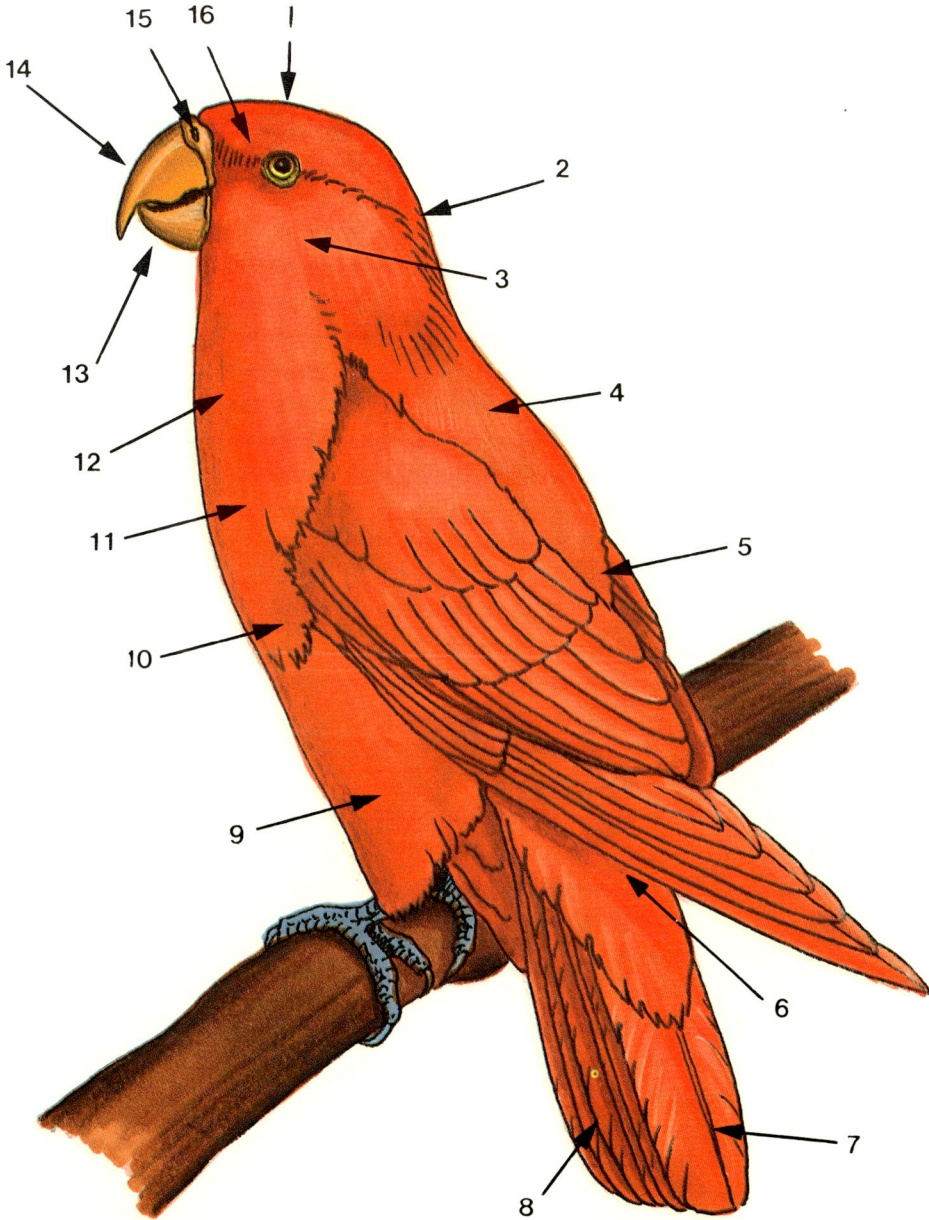

Pair of Black Lories, *Chalcopsitta atra*.

The Genus *Chalcopsitta*

The genus *Chalcopsitta* contains four species of lories. These are among the largest and most stoutly built members of the Loriinae group and among the easiest to keep, faring well on the standard diet of nectar, with plenty of fruit and vegetable matter being offered. However, one note of caution for anyone thinking of obtaining a species of this genus: the voices of these species are strong and harsh, and this should be taken into account if there are neighbors in close proximity, especially as calling often starts at first light when the birds are waiting for their morning feed.

The most noticeable physical characteristic of *Chalcopsitta* lories is the presence of bare skin around the lower mandible.

Black Lory
Chalcopsitta atra

With an overall length of 32cm this is one of the largest of all lories. Nearly the entire plumage of this bird, as its common name suggests, is a shining glossy black. The exceptions are the underside of the tail which is yellow and the area around the rump which becomes a bluish black color. The bill is black, the irides are orange and the legs are grey. Three subspecies are recognized, all being found on Western New Guinea and adjacent islands.

C. a. atra. The nominate race is as described above and almost certainly accounts for just about all the Black Lories widely kept and bred by aviculturists around the world. It is widespread on Western New Guinea and the outlying islands of Batanta and Salawati.

C. a. insignis. This race, commonly known as the Rajah, or Red-quilled, Lory, varies considerably from the nominate by the presence of red quills appearing through the black plumage around the forehead, lores and cheeks. The bend of the wing is violet, with the breast also being violet but streaked with yellow. The area around the rump is a much more distinct blue, and the underwing coverts and thighs are marked with red. All of this coloring is absent on *C. a. atra.* This race is exceptionally rare, although some captive breeding has been attempted in America. Its range is western New Guinea and the adjacent island of Amberpon;

also the Onin and Bomberai peninsulas.

C. a. bernsteini. This race is commonly known as Bernstein's Lory. It differs from the nominate race by having reddish purple markings on the forehead and thighs. It also has a more distinct blue coloring around the rump. There is some argument as to the validity of this race. Few individuals have ever been kept in captivity, and those that have showed changeability in coloration according to age. In the wild this race is confined to the island of Misool and the area around Irian Jaya.

Black lories are normally robust and active aviary inhabitants that adjust well to captivity if wild caught; they show much confidence and character. Often individuals may well become favorites within a collection, regularly flying onto the keeper's arm as he approaches with food. Once settled, they are usually willing breeders, and providing there is indeed a true pair, breeding should occur. Cocks can become particularly aggressive when attempting to breed, and extra care should be taken with this and other large lory species to ensure that they cannot grab toes or limbs of birds

Black Lory, *Chalcopsitta atra.* Bare skin around the lower mandible is one of the characters of this genus.

in adjoining aviaries if they are only separated by a single layer of wire.

The normal-sized clutch of two eggs is incubated for twenty-five days. Youngsters leave the nest box after ten to twelve weeks and are fully independent shortly afterwards.

Duyvenbode's Lory
Chalcopsitta
duivenbodei

Maximum length is 31 cm. The plumage is mainly dark olive brown. The forehead, throat and foreparts of the cheeks are yellow. Breast feathers are also tipped with yellow, with the nape and neck having yellow streaking. The bend of the wing is a golden yellow. The thighs and underwing coverts are an orangy yellow as are markings on the outer tail feathers. The rump is a violet blue color. The bill is black, the iris is red and the legs are dark grey. No subspecies of this lory are recognized, though it is widespread across northern New Guinea, although mainly found at lower altitudes.

The Duyvenbode's Lory, although known in aviculture for some time, has not until comparatively recently become established. It is not a rare species in the wild and proves relatively easy to adjust to captivity. Cock birds

A Duyvenbode's Lory, *Chalcopsitta duivenbodei*, housed in a spacious flight.

can, as with the preceding species, become extremely aggressive,
and it is not unknown for a frus-
trated bird that has been subjected to too much disturbance to
vent his frustration on the eggs or
chicks in the nest box. The temptation to check the nest box too
frequently must be resisted,
particularly if it is the pair's first
attempt at nesting. Two eggs are
again normal, with incubation
taking about twenty-four days.
The chicks fledge at about ten
weeks of age.

This Yellow-streaked Lory, *Chalcopsitta sintillata*, has gnawed some of the bark from its perch.

Yellow-streaked Lory
Chalcopsitta sintillata

Maximum length is 31cm. The forehead, lores, thighs and under-wing coverts are scarlet red. The nape, ear coverts and bill are black, with the rest of the body being an olive brown with yellow streaking. The abdomen is green, as are the upper wing feathers which also have a yellow band running across them. The tail is green, irides are orange to red, and the legs are dark grey. Three subspecies are widely recognized, although with coloration varying so much from one individual to another all are arguable but particularly the third. All are from southern New Guinea and the Aru Islands.

C. s. sintillata. The nominate race is as described above and comes from southern New Guinea.

C. s. rubrifrons. This race varies from the nominate race by having wider and more orangish breast streaking. It is confined to the Aru Islands.

C. s. chloroptera. This race varies little from the nominate other than the breast streaking being slightly narrower. Its range of southern New Guinea overlaps with *C. s. sintillata* with which it intergrades. It is arguable whether this race is distinct.

The Yellow-streaked Lory has long been established in captivity and is the most commonly kept species of *Chalcopsitta*. They prove willing breeders, with the two eggs taking twenty-six days to hatch, although some reports state an incubation period of twenty-four days. The newly hatched chicks spend up to twelve weeks in the nest box before fledging and becoming independent.

Cardinal Lory
Chalcopsitta cardinalis

Maximum length is 31cm. The main body plumage is red, which gets darker and more brownish on the back and wing feathers. Feathers on the underparts are tipped with yellow. The bill is red, fading to black on the upper mandible. Irides are reddish orange, and the legs are dark grey. No subspecies are recognized of this lory, which is found primarily on the Solomon Islands but also on islands in the Tanga, Lihir and Tabor groups.

This species is highly endangered and hitherto has been virtually unknown in aviculture, apart from being kept at the San Diego Zoo. However, in 1990 the Solomon Islands allowed a small number of Cardinal Lories to be exported. These birds have settled well and have begun to breed in several collections in Europe. It is hoped that this bird will in time become more widely established. Incubation time is 24 days, and the youngsters take up to 10 weeks to fledge.

The Cardinal Lory, *Chalcopsitta cardinalis*, is seldom seen in captivity.

Of the *Chalcopsitta* lories, the Yellow-streaked is the most common in aviculture.

The Red Lory, *Eos bornea*, is the most familiar member of the this genus.

The Genus *Eos*

The genus *Eos* contains six species. None are sexually dimorphic; they differ from species of *Chalcopsitta* principally by having no bare skin surrounding the lower mandible. At least four of the species are well known in aviculture and have been kept and bred for a number of years.

Red Lory
Eos bornea

Maximum length is 31cm. Most of the plumage is light red. The primaries are black with a red speculum, and secondaries are tipped with black. The greater wing coverts are edged with black, and the underwing coverts are blue. The tail is reddish brown above and a dull red below. The bill is dark orange, irides are red and the legs are gray. Four subspecies are recognized, although the first three differ as adults only in slight size differences and so in captivity they are almost impossible to identify with certainty. Only the fourth race, from Buru, can easily be recognized by its slightly darker coloration. The four subspecies are found on various islands in Indonesia.

E. b. bornea. The nominate race is as described above and is found on Amboina and Saparua islands.

E. b. rothschildi. This race differs from the nominate only by being slightly smaller. It is confined to the island of Ceram.

E. b. bernsteini. This race differs from the nominate by being slightly larger. It can be found on the Kai Islands.

E. b. cyanonothus. This is the most distinctive race, varying from the other three by virtue of its darker red coloration over its body. It is found only on the island of Buru.

The Red Lory is well established in aviculture, although some confusion surrounds the first three races, with all being commonly known as the Moluccan Red Lory; only the last race is known differently, as the Buru Red Lory. Most of the Moluccan Red Lories seen in aviculture are probably the nominate race *E. b. bornea*. These and the Buru Red Lory have both been successfully kept and bred for a number of years. The needs of these lories are simple; a basic diet of nectar and fruit will keep them happy and in good health. If a true and compatible pair can be found, breeding should follow. The clutch

size is nearly always two, which take twenty-four days to hatch. The newly hatched young spend about nine weeks in the nest box before fledging.

Black-winged Lory
Eos cyanogenia

Maximum length is 30cm. The main body plumage is red. There is a very vivid bluish purple band from the eyes, reaching back over the ear coverts. Black spots are present on the flanks. The upper wing coverts, scapulars and primaries are also black. Thighs and central tail feathers are black. The bill is orange, irides are red and the legs are gray. No subspecies are recognized of this lory, which is found off the coast of Irian Jaya on islands in the Geelvink Bay area but not on mainland New Guinea.

The Black-winged Lory is a highly attractive species that has been known in aviculture for many years. Despite this, it has not until recently become firmly established, as in the past it was imported in small numbers and even with initial success it remained a rarity in captive collections. Breeding nowadays takes place regularly with the clutch size being two eggs taking twenty-six days to incubate, and the young staying in the nest box for up to eleven weeks.

A recently fledged Black-winged Lory, *Eos cyanogenia*.

Blue-streaked Lory
Eos reticulata

Maximum length is 31cm. The main plumage is red. A purple blue band extends from the eyes back to the mantle; the mantle is also streaked with blue. The back down to the rump is a darker shade of red, and both areas are also streaked with blue. The primaries, secondaries and greater wing coverts are all tipped with black. The tail is black above and red below, the bill is bright orange, irides are orange to red and the legs are gray. No subspecies are recognized of this lory; it is mainly found on the Tanimbar island group in Indonesia although it has now been introduced into the Damar and Kai island groups.

The Blue-streaked Lory has over the last ten years become one of the most widely kept species in aviculture, even rivaling the Dusky Lory and the Rainbow Lorikeet in popularity. It is to many people the most strikingly colored and beautiful of the easily available species for a novice to begin with. They also prove prolific breeders. The two eggs are incubated for twenty-six days, but the chicks spend a fairly long period in the nest box, up to twelve or even fourteen weeks. Occasionally parent birds can

A Blue-streaked Lory, *Eos reticulata*, sampling a nectar mix containing fruit.

become unreliable in the latter part of this period, and if a first chick is lost towards the end of its time in the nest box a closer eye should be kept to ensure following chicks are fed properly during this period. The nest box will also require a closer eye with respect to hygiene because of this long rearing period.

Violet-naped Lory
Eos squamata

Maximum length is 27cm. The main plumage is red. A violet collar extends around the neck, giving the lory its common name; this collar is however highly variable not only between different races but even from individual to individual. The abdomen and undertail coverts are purple. The scapulars are a duller purple and are tipped with black. The greater wing coverts and flight feathers are marginated and tipped with black. The tail is purple red above and a dull red below. The bill is orange to red, irides are a yellowish orange and the legs are gray. Three subspecies are recognized, being spread across the Western Papuan islands, Irian Jaya, the Maju Islands, Weda Islands and northern Moluccas in Indonesia.

E. s. squamata. The nominate race is as described as above and occurs on the Schildpad Islands

In the wake of increased importation, in recent years the Blue-streaked Lory, *Eos reticulata*, has been widely bred.

A Violet-naped Lory, *Eos squamata*, perched in front of its nest box.

and on Gebe, Waigeu, Batanta and Misool in the Western Papuan Islands.

E. s. riciniata. This race differs from the nominate by having a more prominent violet gray collar which extends up to the hindcrown. It also has red scapulars. It is found on Weda Islands and on the islands of the northern Moluccas.

E. s. obiensis. This race differs from the nominate by lacking the distinctive purple markings over the upper body. Called the Obi Lory, it is found only on Obi Island in the northern Moluccas. Many people think this form is a distinct species.

The Violet-naped Lory is well established in aviculture and is a willing breeder, although in the past some interbreeding of the subspecies has taken place. These are beautifully marked lories which provide their keepers with few problems but much enjoyment. Breeding takes place regularly, with the clutch of two eggs being incubated for twenty-six days. Chicks generally then spend up to eleven weeks in the nest box before fledging, and if problems do occur in the latter stages, as with the previous species, extra care may be needed with respect to nest-box hygiene, rearing diet, and checking to ensure the chick is in fact being fed.

Red-and-blue Lory
Eos histrio

Maximum length is 31cm. The main plumage is red, which becomes darker towards the rump. A purple band extends across the hindcrown with slightly more bluish lines reaching from the eyes to the mantle; the mantle itself and back are purple blue. Scapulars, flight feathers and thighs are black, with wing coverts also being tipped with black. The underparts are red with a blue band running across the breast. The undertail coverts are tipped with blue. The tail is reddish purple above and red below. The bill is a deep orange, irides are red and the legs are gray. Three subspecies are recognized, all coming from Indonesia.

E. h. histrio. The nominate race is as described above and comes from Sangir and Siao islands.

E. h. talautensis. This race differs from the nominate by being less black on the wing coverts and flight feathers. It is restricted to the Talaud Islands.

E. h. challengeri. This race differs from the nominate by the blue band on the breast being smaller and less well defined. The blue line from the eye does not extend fully to the mantle. It is also noticeably smaller than the nominate, being only 25cm in total length. This race is found only on Nerusa Island.

The camera elicits a forthright stare from this Red Lory, *Eos bornea.*

The Red-and-blue Lory is virtually unknown in aviculture with only *E. h. challengeri,* commonly known as Challenger's Lory, being kept in the past. Very little information is available, but general care for this species is the same as in other *Eos* species, and it is thought that breeding is also very similar to other *Eos* species.

Blue-eared Lory
Eos semilarvata

Also known as the Ceram Lory, the maximum length is 24cm. The main plumage is red with a violet blue patch covering the upper cheeks, ear coverts and extending down the sides of the neck, giving the lory its common name. The abdomen and under tail coverts are also blue. The primaries are black, secondaries are red tipped with black and the tail is brownish red above and a duller red below. The bill is orange, irides are a reddish orange and the legs are gray. No subspecies are recognized of this lory, which is restricted to the mountains of central Ceram in Indonesia.

The Blue-eared Lory is little known in aviculture, and again I am not aware of any captive breeding having taken place or of any relevant field observations of breeding.

The Red-and-blue Lory, *Eos histrio*, has seldom become available to aviculturists

A Dusky Lory, *Pseudeos fuscata*, perched beside the entrance to its nest box.

The Genus *Pseudeos*

The genus *Pseudeos* contains only one species which is very closely related to those of *Eos* but varies by the tail being noticeably smaller, and there is bare skin surrounding the lower mandible, which is not the case in *Eos* lories.

Dusky Lory
Pseudeos fuscata

Maximum length is 25cm. The shades of coloration in this species are highly variable. The main plumage is a dusky olive brown. The crown is dull yellow. Feathers of the hindneck and upper breast are brown tipped with yellow. There is a yellowish orange band reaching across the foreneck, with a second, less well-defined band lower down across the breast; the lower breast and abdomen are also yellowish orange. The back and rump are white. Thighs are orange or red. The underwing coverts are brown and dull yellow with two orange bands running across the underside of the flight feathers. The tail is yellow marked with orange, with the undertail coverts being dark blue. The bill is dark orange. Irides are red and the legs are gray. No subspecies are recognized from this lory, which is widespread across New Guinea and on Salawati in the Papuan Islands and on Japen Island in Geelvink Bay.

Although no subspecies are recognized and coloration is highly variable, there are two distinct color phases, known as the "yellow" and "orange" phases. The orange color gene is the dominant one, with orange parents always producing orange young, while yellow parents can produce young of either color phase.

The Dusky Lory in recent times has probably been the most widely kept and bred Loriinae species in aviculture. Captive-bred birds are easily available and are among the best choices for a first species to keep. Steady captive-bred birds prove willing and reliable breeders, often having two or more clutches every year. The normal clutch of two eggs are incubated for twenty-four days, with young chicks staying in the nest box for about ten weeks before emerging.

Two Chattering Lories of the yellow-backed subspecies, *Lorius garrulus flavopalliatus*, in an aviary.

The Genus *Lorius*

The genus *Lorius* contains six species; all are medium-sized, stocky birds with the most distinctive feature of these birds being the slightly broader and less-pointed bill. None of these species are sexually dimorphic. All *Lorius* species make excellent aviary inhabitants, proving hardy, lively, confident, and full of character. Their dietary needs are simple; they fare well on a standard diet of nectar mix with plenty of fruit and vegetable matter. Sexing has been a problem in the past, but when true, compatible pairs can be obtained, then breeding normally follows with few problems.

Chattering Lory
Lorius garrulus

Maximum length is 30cm. The main plumage is red, with a darker red on the scapulars. The thighs and wings are green; the bend of the wing and the upper wing coverts are yellow. There is a broad red band running across the underside of the primaries. The tail is red, tipped with dark green. The bill is orange; irides are orange to red, and the legs are gray.

Three subspecies are recognized for this lory, all coming from the Moluccan Islands in Indonesia.

L. g. garrulus. The nominate race is as described above and is found on Halmahera and the Weda Islands.

L. g. flavopalliatus. This race differs from the nominate race by having a bright yellow patch on the mantle and by having a brighter green color on the wings. It can be found on the islands of Batjan and Obi.

L. g. morotaianus. This race is similar to *L. g. flavopalliatus*, but the yellow patch on the mantle and the green on the wing is of a slightly duller color. This race occurs on the islands of Moratai and Raou.

The Chattering Lory has long been well established in captivity. The nominate race is not the most commonly available of the subspecies, but it is available from time to time and is easily distinguishable by the lack of yellow on the mantle. The latter two subspecies both sometimes fall under the common name of the Yellow-backed Lory, although most of these lories are probably *L. g.*

A Black-capped Lory, *Lorius lory*, hangs on the aviary wire.

flavopalliatus. This is the most commonly available of the subspecies. All subspecies have been bred and are known to be reliable parents usually, with breeding often being continual, even through the winter. The normal clutch size is two eggs, which take twenty-six days to incubate, and the chicks remain in the nest box for a period of about ten weeks before fledging.

Black-capped Lory
Lorius lory

Maximum length is 31cm. The main plumage is red. The forehead, lores, crown and nape are black. There is a dark blue band on the hindneck. the mantle is blue and the wings are green. The undertail coverts, thighs, abdo-

Like other members of the genus, the Black-capped Lory, *Lorius lory*, is a confiding aviary subject.

men and lower breast are blue, which extends up the sides of the breast to meet the mantle. The underwing coverts are red with a yellow band stretching across the undersides of the flight feathers. The tail is red, tipped with black above and olive yellow below. The cere is gray. The bill is light orange. Irides are yellow and the legs are gray. Six subspecies are recognized of this lory, all coming from New Guinea and the Papuan Islands.

L. l. lory. The nominate race is as described above and occurs on Waigeu, Batanta, Salawati and Misool in the western Papuan Islands. Also on the Vogelkop, Irian Jaya.

L. l. erythrothorax. This race differs from the nominate by the absence of blue on the sides of the

Above and Below: The subspecies *erythrothorax* of the Black-capped Lory, *Lorius lory*.

breast. The blue band on the back of the neck is also narrower than in the nominate form. This race occurs in the southern part of Geelvink Bay and from the Onin Peninsula, Irian Jaya, east to southeastern Papua New Guinea.

L. l. somu. This race is similar to *L. l. erythrothorax* but lacks completely the blue on the hindneck. This race can be found in southern New Guinea.

L. l. salvordorii. This race is also similar to *L. l. erythrothorax* but has a well-defined blue band on the hindneck. The underwing coverts are a darker blue, and the lower breast and abdomen are almost black, which extends to the underwing coverts. This race is found in northeastern New Guinea.

L. l. viridicrissalis. This race is similar to *L. l. salvordorii* but has a darker, almost black, blue band on the hindneck. This race is from northern New Guinea.

L. l. cyanuchen. This race is also similar to *L. l. salvordorii* but lacks the red on the nape. The blue on the hindneck extends up to meet the back of the crown. This race is found on Biak Island in Geelvink Bay and also in Irian Jaya.

The Black-capped Lory has always been popular and much sought after in aviculture. Despite this, it has failed to become established and, when available, commands a high price. Breeding has occurred in the past, although not in any large numbers. There is also some variance in the reports of the incubation time. These can vary from twenty-three to twenty-six days; the most consistent time appears to be twenty-five days. The chicks usually then take about nine weeks before fledging, with normally no problems being reported.

The Purple-capped Lory, *Lorius domicellus*, is seldom seen in aviculture. While also uncommon within its restricted Indonesian range, reports indicate that is a popular pet among people there.

Purple-capped Lory
Lorius domicellus

Maximum length is 28cm. The main plumage is red, which becomes darker on the back. The forehead, lores and crown are black. A purple patch borders the black cap, giving this lory its common name. A yellow band runs across the upper breast. Thighs are violet blue. The wings are green with the bends of the wings being white with blue markings. Upper wing coverts are blue, and a yellow band reaches across the underside of the flight feathers. The tail is red, becoming brown towards the tip. The bill is orange. Irides are reddish brown and the legs are gray. No subspecies are recognized of this lory, which is found on the islands of Ceram and Amboina in Indonesia.

The Purple-capped Lory is rare in captivity but breeding does take place. The normal-sized clutch of two eggs is incubated for twenty-four days, with young birds spending up to twelve weeks in the nest box before fledging.

A captive Purple-capped Lory, *Lorius domicellus*, poses amid a spray of flowers.

Purple-bellied Lory
Lorius hypoinochrous

The maximum length is 26cm. The main plumage is red; the breast is lighter than the upper abdomen, while the lower abdomen and thighs are purple. The forehead, lores, crown and nape are black. The underwing coverts are red, with the outermost feathers being tipped with black. The tail is red, tipped with bluish green above and dull yellow below. The bill is orange, irides are orange to red, and the legs are gray.

Three subspecies are recognized for this lory, all coming from southeastern New Guinea and the Papuan Islands.

L. h. hypoinochrous. The nominate race is as described above and is found on Misima and Tagula in the Papuan Islands.

L. h. rosselianus. This race differs from the nominate by the red on the breast being the same shade as that of the upper abdomen. This race is only found on Rossel Island.

L. h. devittatus. This race differs from the nominate by lacking the black edging on the outermost underwing covert feathers. It can be found in southern New Guinea and also on Trobriand in the Woodlark Islands.

The Purple-bellied Lory is little known in aviculture, and I am not aware of any captive breeding having taken place. It is unlikely, though, to vary much from other *Lorius* species, with reports of its general care being much the same as that for other species. It is assumed that incubation takes 26 days and the young fledge after 11 weeks.

Yellow-bibbed Lory
Lorius chlorocercus

Maximum length is 28cm. The main plumage is red. The forehead, lores and crown are black. There are also black patches on either side of the neck. There is a yellow band running across the upper breast which is better defined than in the Purple-capped Lory, giving this species its common name. The thighs are violet and the wings are green. The bend of the wing is white with blue markings. The underwing coverts are blue, and a broad red band reaches across the undersides of the primaries. The tail is red, tipped with dull green above and a dull yellow below. The bill is dark orange with a dark patch at the base of the upper mandible. Irides are orange and the legs are gray. No subspecies are recognized for this lory, which is found in the Eastern Solomon islands.

This species again is extremely rare. Although breeding has not bee widespread, it is known that incubation takes 25 days and that the young fledge after 11 weeks. There are reports of mealworms being particularly sought after by parent birds for feeding to young chicks, but otherwise they should be maintained on a nectar diet with fruit and vegetable matter.

For this Yellow-bibbed Lory, *Lorius chlorocercus*, a nest box has been installed in the back corner of the aviary.

White-naped Lory
Lorius albidinuchus

Maximum length is 26cm. The main plumage is red. The forehead, lores and crown are black, with a white patch on the hindneck providing the common name. There are faint yellow markings on either side of the upper breast. The wings are green, except for the underwing coverts which are red, and a yellow band that reaches across the flight feathers. The tail is red tipped with green above and red tipped with yellow below. The bill is orange with a dark patch at the base of the upper mandible. Irides are yellow and the legs are a grayish black. No subspecies are recognized from this lory, which comes from New Ireland in the Bismark Archipelago.

The White-naped Lory is virtually unknown in aviculture and is highly unlikely ever to appear. As with the previous species, little information is available on its care and breeding.

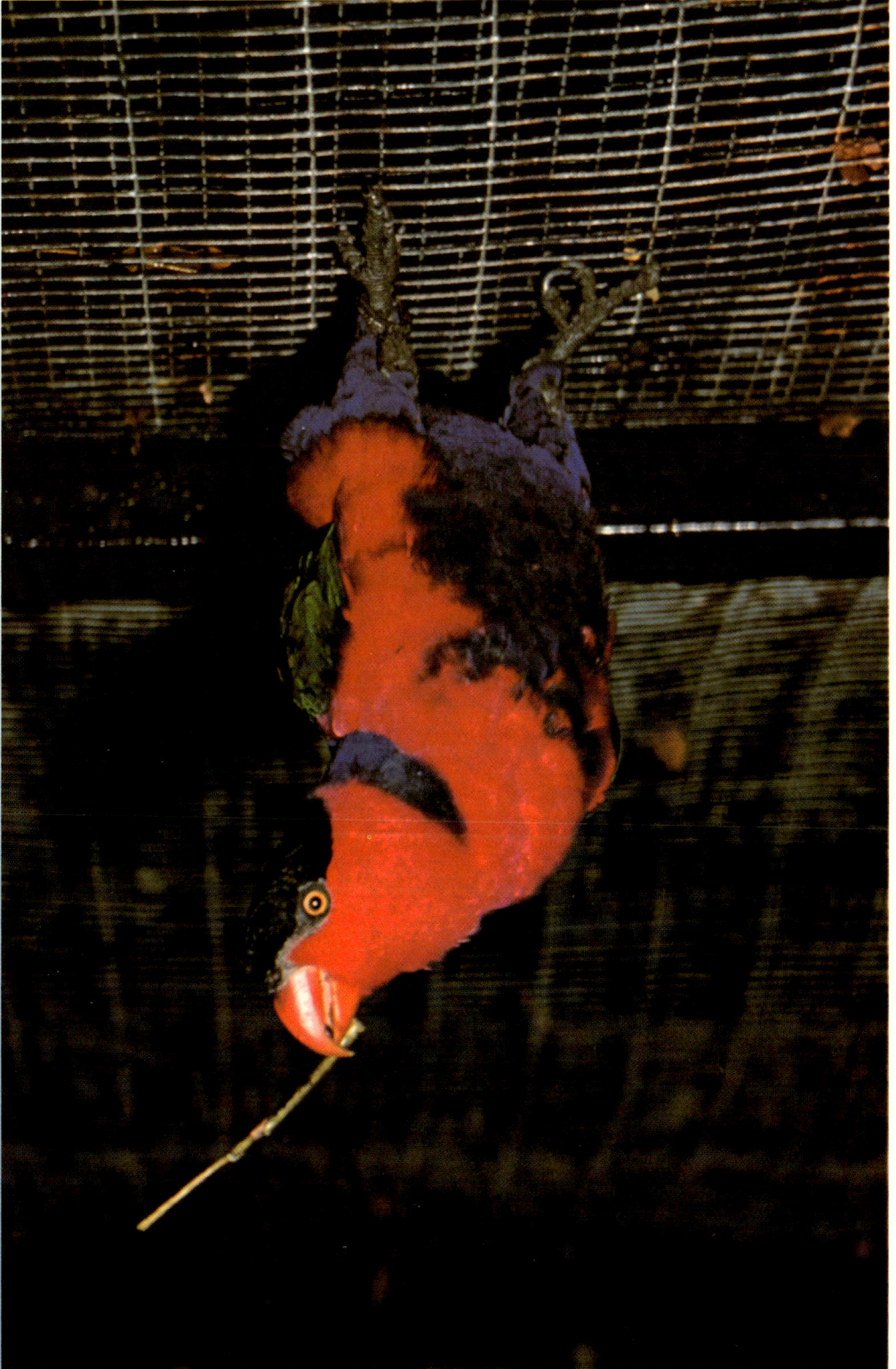

An acrobatic Black-capped Lory, *Lorius lory*, hangs from the wire roof of the flight.

The Blue-crowned Lory, *Vini australis*.

The Genus *Vini*

The genus *Vini* contains five species; all are small, stoutly built birds that are mainly isolated in small island populations. As such they have suffered more than most from the introduction of non-native predators and deforestation, which have made all five species highly endangered. None are ever likely to be widely available in aviculture. The most well-known species of the group, the Tahiti Blue Lory, has been the focus of a concentrated breeding program by San Diego Zoo and several private aviculturists.

the legs, and the iris is yellow. No subspecies are recognized, with the wild population being limited to Samoa and Tonga islands, with smaller populations also being found on several small nearby islands.

This species is virtually unknown in aviculture although it has been exhibited by Walsrode Bird Park in Germany and by San Diego Zoo in America. San Diego managed to successfully breed this species during the early 1970s, and recorded an incubation period of twenty three days.

Blue-crowned Lory
Vini australis

Maximum length is 19cm. The main body plumage is green, which becomes paler and brighter around the hindneck and the rump. The lores, ear coverts, throat and the abdominal patch are red. The thighs and lower abdomen are purple blue. The crown is a darker blue but with mauve blue streaking, which gives the bird its common name. The underside of the tail is a more yellowish green than on the rest of the body. The bill is orange, as are

Kuhl's Lory
Vini kuhlii

Maximum length is 19cm. The upper parts of the body are green, which becomes more yellowish over the back towards the rump. The crown is streaked with a paler shade of green. The green of the crown is separated from the back by a bluish purple band around the occiput, connecting with the throat on either side. The under-parts of the body are bright scarlet and the thighs are purple. The undersides of the wings are green. The tail is scarlet above and grayish below, with greenish yellow on the undertail coverts. The bill is orange, the iris is red and the legs are a brownish orange. No subspecies are recognized of this lory which is restricted to the island of Rimitara in the Tubuai Island group. Occasional birds have been seen elsewhere in the Tubuai Islands, most often on Tubuai Island itself. These are mainly credited with being escaped captive birds, so with the main population being confined to one island this species is highly vulnerable to any deforestation or the attentions of an introduced predator. Although it has occasionally been seen in aviculture in the past, it has never become established and no significant captive populations exist.

Stephen's Lory
Vini stepheni

Maximum length is 19cm. Superficially similar to the Kuhl's Lory, the upper parts are green which becomes more yellowish towards the rump. The crown is also streaked with a lighter green. This species, however, lacks the purple blue occiput that is so noticeable in the preceding species. The underparts are scarlet, although there is a broken band of green and purple reaching across the breast. The lower abdomen and thighs are purple. The underwing coverts are red and green. The tail is yellowish green. The bill is orange, as are the legs, and the iris is yellow. No

subspecies are recognized of this lory, which occurs only on Henderson Island in the Pitcairn Island group.

The Stephen's Lory is unknown in aviculture, and there are very few reports of its habits in the wild, none of which relate to its breeding behavior.

Ultramarine Lory
Vini ultramarina

The maximum length is 18cm. The forehead is a rich blue, becoming mauve over the crown and occiput, with lighter streaking. The upper parts are a dullish blue which is paler around the rump. The underparts by comparison are white with dark blue markings. There is a dark blue band across the breast. Thighs and undertail coverts are mauve blue; the underwing coverts are dull blue. The tips of the blue tail feathers are white. Bill is brown with orange at the base of the upper mandible; the iris is a yellowish orange and the legs are also orange. No subspecies are recognized of this lory, which inhabits the Marquesas Islands.

The Ultramarine Lory is extremely rare in captivity today but has appeared from time to time in the past. Successful breeding has been achieved, and although reports vary, incubation time is twenty-five days, with young fledging about eight weeks after hatching. It is also clear from past reports that this species is very delicate and requires sensitive

Nestling Blue-crowned Lory, *Vini australis*, one of the youngsters bred at the San Diego Zoo.

care, if a keeper is ever lucky enough to care for one.

Tahiti Blue Lory
Vini peruviana

Maximum length is 18cm. The main plumage is a dark mauve blue, which on the crown is streaked with a paler blue. The ear coverts, throat and upper breast by contrast are white. The bill is orange, irides are yellow and the legs are yellowish orange. No subspecies are recognized of this lory, which is found on the Society Islands and western-most Tuamotu Islands.

The Tahiti Blue Lory is well known as one of the rarest and most beautiful of lories; its simple color scheme deserves the latter description, while the fact of its rarity is sadly without doubt. If a poll was taken amongst lory keepers as to which species they would most like to keep, this species would surely top the list. Most information on the care and breeding in captivity is gained from the on-going breeding program at San Diego Zoo. Breeding has been achieved regularly, and it is known that the incubation time is twenty-five days; the young chicks do not become independent for at least thirteen weeks.

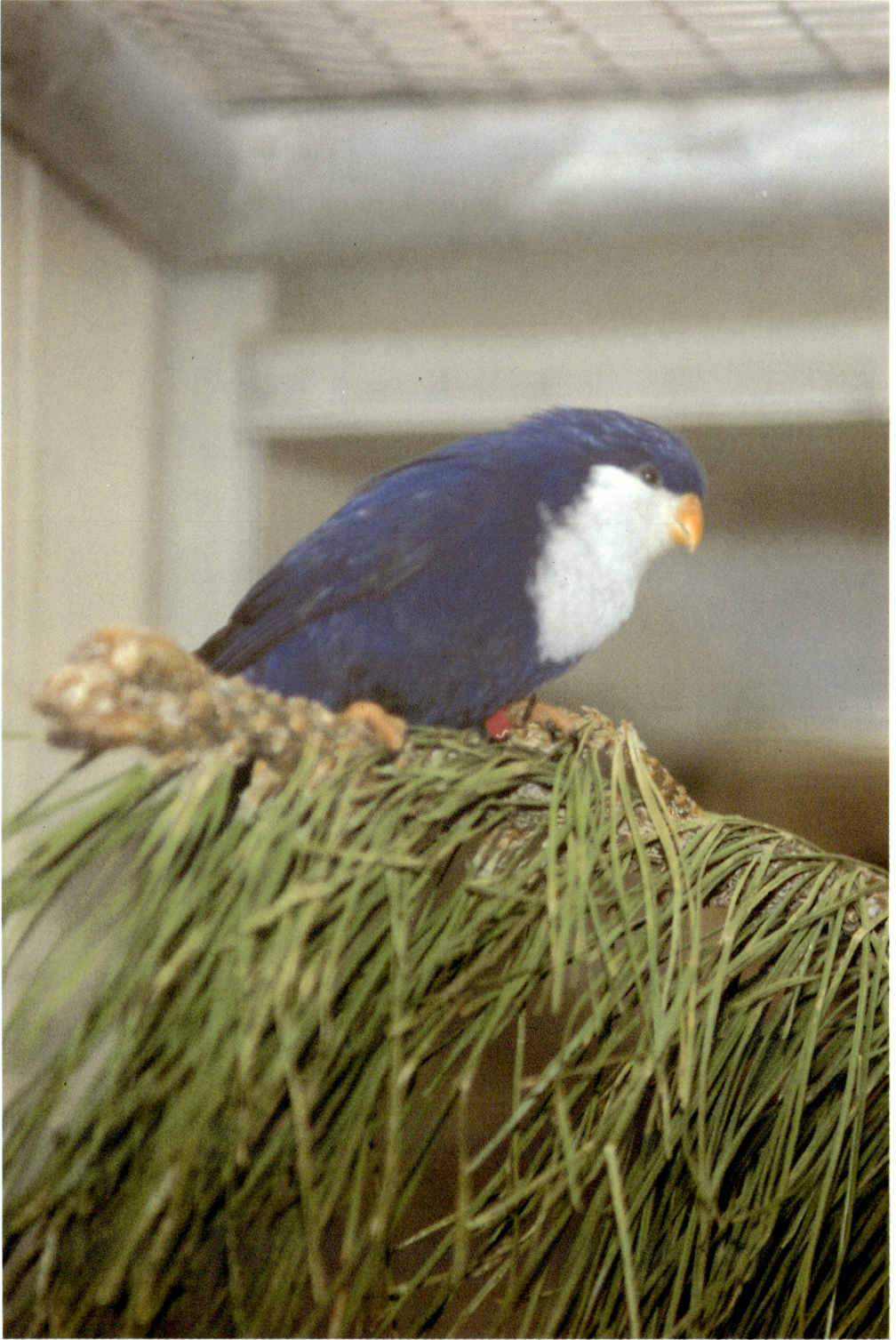

The Tahiti Blue Lory, *Vini peruviana*.

The Genus *Phigys*

The genus *Phigys* is monotypic, containing only one species which is probably an offshoot of *Vini*. This species is slightly stockier than the *Vini* species and there is a slight sexual dimorphism. The most distinctive feature, however, is the presence of elongated feathers covering the hindneck, forming a nuchal collar.

Solitary Lory
Phigys solitarius

Also known as the Collared, or Ruffed, Lory. Overall length is 20cm. The forehead, lores and crown are dark purple; in the female the forehead is paler and the hindcrown is tinged with green. The back, wings and tail are green, with the rump being a brighter yellowish green. The ear coverts, cheeks and area from the throat to the upper abdomen are scarlet. The thighs and lower abdomen are deep purple. The underwing and tail coverts are green. The bill is orange, irides are orange to red, and the legs are a pinkish orange. No subspecies are recognized from this monotypic species, which is found on the larger islands of the Fiji group.

The Solitary Lory, although common and quite conspicuous over much of the woodland and forest regions of its natural range, has never been common in captivity and is extremely rare in aviculture. There is one report of captive breeding and a small amount of information from field observation. These suggest that the normal clutch size is two eggs. These are incubated for about thirty days, and the chicks then take a further nine weeks to fledge.

Billing between two Solitary Lories, *Phigys solitarius*.

The nominate form of the Rainbow Lorikeet, _Trichoglossus haematodus haematodus_.

The Genus *Trichoglossus*

The genus *Trichoglossus* contains ten species, although with twenty subspecies of the Rainbow Lorikeet alone there is some debate as to whether many of these deserve to be treated as full species. Species of this genus are medium-sized lorikeets with gradated tails made up of elongated, narrow, pointed feathers; there is also no area of bare skin around the base of the lower mandible. Most if not all species adapt well to captivity; although many of the species in this group are unlikely ever to become widely available, dietary-wise they fare well on the standard nectar-and-fruit combination, and once properly acclimatized, they usually prove extremely hardy aviary birds.

Rainbow Lorikeet
Trichoglossus haematodus

With twenty, sometimes quite distinct, races, many common names are used for different races. These include Green-naped, Mitchell's, Forsten's, Edward's, Wetar, Rosenberg's, Coconut, Red-collared, and Swainson's. It is not surprising then that this is probably the most argued-about species of Loriinae. Overall length is normally around 26cm, unless otherwise stated in the subspecies descriptions. The forehead, lores and chin are a bluish mauve, with the rest of the head being brownish black, with a yellowish collar reaching around the back of the neck. The breast feathers are red with the tips being edged with black. The lower abdomen is dark green. The thighs and undertail coverts are yellow marked with green. The rest of the underparts are also green. The underwing coverts are orange with a yellow band reaching across the underside of the flight feathers. The tail is green above and dull yellow below. Bill is a reddish orange, irides are red and the legs are greenish gray. Twenty subspecies are recognized, ranging through Indonesia, New Guinea and Australia.

T. h. haematodus. The nominate race, often known as the Green-naped Lorikeet, is as described above. It is without doubt the most commonly seen race, being widespread from western New Guinea, Geelvink Bay, Buru, Amboina, Ceram, Ceramlaut,

Rainbow Lorikeet, *Trichoglossus haematodus*, this being the subspecies *forsteni*.

A Rainbow Lorikeet *Trichoglossus haematodus moluccanus* housed in a collection with other lories.

Goram, Watubela and the Western Papuan Islands.

T. h. mitchellii. This race, commonly known as Mitchell's Lorikeet, varies from the nominate by being slightly smaller. The breast is light red and the lower abdomen is black. The most distinctive difference, however, is that the collar around the back of the neck is also red. This race is found on Bali and Lombok in Indonesia.

T. h. forsteni. This race, commonly known as Forsten's Lorikeet, is similar to *T. h. mitchellii* but differs by the lower abdomen being purple, the collar being more yellowish, and the forehead and cheeks being streaked with violet blue. This race is restricted to Sumbawa.

T. h. djampeanus. This race race is similar to *T. h. forsteni* but differs by the head being darker and with much more distinctive blue streaking. There is dark purple on the hindneck below the collar and no dark tipping on the uniformly red breast. This race is restricted to Djampea Island.

T. h. stresemanni. This race is also similar to *T. h. forsteni* but differs by the breast being more orange. It also has yellow bases on the mantle feathers and the occiput is tinged with green. This race is restricted to Kalao Tua.

T. h. fortis. This race differs from the nominate race by the forehead and cheeks being streaked with blue. The lores, throat, line of the eye and occiput are all green. The breast is yellow-ish orange. The abdomen is dark green and the underwing coverts are yellow. This race is found on the Sumba Islands.

T. h. weberi. This race, commonly known as Weber's Lorikeet, is smaller than the nominate race. The main plumage is green, the breast is marked with yellow and the forehead is washed with blue. This race is only found on Flores.

T. h. capistratus. This race, commonly known as Edward's Lorikeet, differs from the nominate by the head being green. The forehead, forecrown and cheeks are streaked with blue. The breast is yellow with no orange marking. The collar is wider and greenish yellow. The abdomen is dark green and the underwing coverts are yellow marked with orange. This race is found on the island of Timor.

T. h. flavotectus. This race, commonly known as the Wetar Lorikeet, is similar to *T. h.*

Two chicks of the *forsteni* subspecies of the Rainbow Lorikeet, *Trichoglossus haematodus*, fifty-three days old.

Rainbow Lorikeet *Trichoglossus haematodus capistratus.*

The subspecies *Trichoglossus haematodus moluccanus* is often called Swainson's Lorikeet.

capistratus but the breast is lighter and without orange marking. The orange marking is also absent from the underwing coverts. This form occurs on the islands of Wetar and Roma.

T. h. rosenbergii. This race, commonly known as Rosenberg's Lorikeet, is similar to the nominate race but has a thin red ring running above the yellow collar on the back of the neck. The feathers on the breast are broadly tipped with purple. The abdomen is also purple and there is an orange band running across the underside of the flight feathers. This race is restricted to the island of Biak in Geelvink Bay.

T. h. intermedius. This race differs only slightly from the nominate by having less blue on the head. It is found in the north of New Guinea.

T. h. micropteryx. This race again only differs from the nominate race slightly by the general body plumage being paler and the nuchal patch being more greenish. This race is found on mainland New Guinea and Misma Island.

T. h. massena. This race, commonly known as the Coconut

The brown nape is the most obvious characteristic of the Rainbow Lorikeet subspecies *Trichoglossus haematodus massena*.

Lorikeet, is similar to *T. h. micropteryx* but the collar is less yellow. The nape is tinged with brown and the breast is paler with less-well-defined barring. This race is from the Solomon Islands.

T. h. caeruleiceps. Sometimes referred to as *T. h. nigrogularis,* it is similar to the nominate race but with the crown and sides of the face being light blue. The abdomen is also a blackish green. this race is found on mainland New Guinea and also the Aru and Eastern Kai islands.

T. h. brooki. This race is similar to *T. h. caeruleiceps* but the black

Rainbow Lorikeet *Trichoglossus haematodus weberi.*

on the abdomen is more extensive, with no green present. This race however is known only from a few specimens from Trangan in the Aru Islands.

T. h. flavicans. This race appears to be highly variable with the underparts, undertail coverts and tail all varying from yellow to dull green. The neck collar is yellow. The forehead and lores are violet, with the remainder of the head being black with green streaking. This race is found on New Hanover and the Admiralty Islands.

T. h. nesophilus. This race is similar to *T. h. flavicans* but the underparts, undertail coverts and tail are all green and do not vary towards yellow. It can be found on the Ninigo and Hermit island groups.

T. h. deplanchii. This race is similar to *T. h. massena* but differs by having more blue on the head, less brown on the nape and less yellow on the thighs and undertail coverts. This race occurs on New Caledonia and the Loyalty Islands.

T. h. moluccanus. This race, commonly known as the Swainson's Lorikeet, has a violet blue head. The breast is yellow to light orange, with no barring present. The abdomen is deep purple and the underwing coverts are orange washed with yellow. It occurs across eastern and southeastern Australia and can also be found on Tasmania.

T. h. rubritorquis. This race, commonly known as the Red-collared Lorikeet, differs from the nominate by the throat and foreneck being black with the rest of the head being violet blue. The breast is light orange without barring. The abdomen is greenish black and the collar around the neck is bright red, giving the lorikeet its common name. This race is found on northern mainland Australia.

Rainbow Lorikeets of one form or another have long been established in aviculture and are perhaps the best-known members of the Loriinae subfamily. Breeding has taken place and does so regularly; once settled, all seem to be willing breeders. There is some variation among the different races, but incubation takes between twenty-three and twenty-six days, with the young leaving the nest box eight to twelve weeks after hatching.

Ornate Lorikeet
Trichoglossus ornatus

The maximum length is 25cm. The forehead, crown and upper ear coverts are purple, while the cheeks and lower ear coverts are orange red. A yellow band is present on the sides of the neck behind the ear coverts; the occiput is red with the feathers being tipped with a dusky blue. The throat and breast are orange to red, with feathers being marginated with bluish black, giving a barred effect. The abdomen and vent are green marked with yellow, with the rest of the body being green. Underwing coverts are yellow. The tail is green above

Two birds of the *rubritorquis* subspecies of the Rainbow Lorikeet, *Trichoglossus haematodus*.

and a dull yellow below. The bill and iris are both dark orange and the legs are a greenish gray. No subspecies are recognized for this lorikeet which is found in Indonesia on Sulawesi and outlying islands.

Although well known in aviculture and regularly imported through the years, the Ornate Lorikeet is not as well established in captivity as it should be, and

The Ornate Lorikeet, *Trichoglossus ornatus*.

A Perfect Lorikeet, *Trichoglossus euteles*, in an aviary furnished with tree branches.

would be well deserving of the attention of someone looking to set up several aviaries to concentrate on breeding one species. Breeding has taken place though, with the clutch size being two. The eggs take twenty-six days to incubate, and the young birds stay in the nest box for about nine weeks before fledging.

Cherry-collared Lorikeet
Trichoglossus rubiginosus

This species is also known as the Ponape Lorikeet. Maximum length is 24cm. The main plumage is maroon red with the feathers on the neck and underparts being edged darker, giving a barred effect. The flight and tail feathers are olive yellow. The bill in the male is orange, while that of the female is slightly more yellowish. The irides also show sexual dimorphism, being yellowish orange in the male and grayish white in the female. The legs are gray. No subspecies are recognized in this lorikeet that is found only on Ponape Island in the Caroline island group.

The Cherry-collared Lorikeet is little known in aviculture, and as far as I am aware no captive breeding has taken place. It has been noted from observations of this bird nesting in the wild that, unusually, only one egg is laid per clutch. The wild population is also highly at risk.

Perfect Lorikeet
Trichoglossus euteles

Also known as the Yellow-faced Lorikeet. The maximum length is 25cm. The main plumage is green. The head is olive yellow with a pale green collar around the neck. The breast and upper abdomen are greenish yellow, and there is a yellow band running across the underside of the flight feathers. The undersides of the tail feathers are yellow, with the undertail coverts being green tipped with yellow. The upper side of the tail is green. The bill is orange, irides are red and the legs are gray. No subspecies are recognized in this lorikeet that is found on Timor and the Lesser Sunda Islands.

The Perfect Lorikeet, although frequently available, has failed to become more widely established mainly because its simple coloration is less attractive than in other Loriinae species. However, I find this species to be one of the friendliest and easiest to tame. Another advantage is that its voice is not quite as harsh as many of its relatives. Also, it is adaptable towards food, eating just about any mix of nectar or fruit matter offered to it. Breeding takes place regularly in those collections that keep this species. The clutch size can be up to three eggs, which take twenty-three days to incubate. The young birds usually stay in the nest box for about nine weeks.

A nest site in the form of a hollow log has been prepared for this Scaly-breasted Lorikeet, *Trichoglossus chlorolepidotus*.

The postures of these Yellow-and-green Lorikeets _Trichoglossus flavoviridis meyeri_ suggest that they may be pair-bonding.

Scaly-breasted Lorikeet _Trichoglossus chlorolepidotus_

Maximum length is 23cm. The main plumage is green. The feathers of the neck. throat and breast are yellow broadly marginated with green, giving a scalloped appearance. The undertail coverts, thighs and lower flanks are green strongly marked with yellow. The underwing coverts are orangy red with an orangy red band also extending across the underside of the flight feathers. The bill is deep orange. Irides are yellow to orange and the legs are a grayish brown color. No subspecies are recognized in this lorikeet that can be found on northeastern mainland Australia.

The Scaly-breasted Lorikeet has been rare in aviculture outside Australia, but within its own country its populations are secure and it has been widely kept and bred by bird keepers. The incubation time is known to be twenty-three days, with the young birds staying in the nest box for about eight weeks before they fledge.

Yellow-and-green Lorikeet _Trichoglossus flavoviridis_

One race is also commonly known as Meyer's Lorikeet. Maximum length is 23cm. The main plumage is green, with the feathers of the forehead and crown being olive yellow. The ear coverts, cheek patches and chin are a dusky green with each feather being marginated with yellow. There is a brown nuchal collar, while the throat, breast and upper abdomen are yellow tipped with dark green. The vent and undertail coverts are a greenish yellow, as are the underwing coverts. The tail is green above and a dull yellow below. The bill is orange, irides are yellow to orange and the legs are gray. Two sub-species are recognized, both coming from Indonesia.

T. f. flavoviridis. The nominate race is as described above and can be found on the Sula Islands in Indonesia.

T. f. meyeri. This race, commonly known as Meyer's Lorikeet, differs from the nominate race mainly by being smaller. The hindcrown and nape are more greenish brown, and the breast and upper abdomen feathers are a greenish yellow. This race is found only on Sulawesi.

The nominate race of the Yellow-and-green Lorikeet is virtually unknown in aviculture, and its wild populations are extremely vulnerable. *T. f. meyeri,* although also vulnerable in its wild range, is now quite commonly kept and has been bred. The incubation time is twenty-three days, and the chicks stay in the nest box for around nine weeks before they fledge.

Scaly-breasted Lorikeet, *Trichoglossus chlorolepidotus*. This youngster is still a couple of weeks short of fledging.

Mount Apo Lorikeet
Trichoglossus johnstoniae

Also known as Mrs. Johnstone's, or the Mindanao, Lorikeet. Maximum length is 20cm. The main plumage is green. The forehead, lores and chin are rose red with a purple brown band reaching from the lores to the occiput. There is some yellow on the underside of the secondaries, throat and breast. The abdomen feathers are yellowish green with some being edged more darkly. The tail is green above and olive yellow below. The bill is orangy red. The irides are red and the legs are a greenish gray. No subspecies are recognized, as the form *T. j. pistra* is now widely believed not to vary at all from the nominate race. This species is highly endangered and is confined to the mountains of Mindanao Island in the Philippines.

The Mount Apo Lorikeet is never likely to become well known in aviculture, and what information that is known comes mainly from the records of San Diego Zoo, which maintains and breeds this species. They show that the normal clutch size is two eggs, which are incubated for twenty-three days, and the young may fledge as early as five weeks after hatching.

Facing page: A Mount Apo Lorikeet, *Trichoglossus johnstoniae*, in the San Diego Zoo.

Iris Lorikeet
Trichoglossus iris

Maximum length is 20cm. The main body plumage is green, more yellowish on the underparts and underwing coverts. The forehead, forecrown and area behind the eye are reddish orange. In the female the forecrown is green marked with red. There is a reddish violet band from the eyes to the hindneck. The occiput is grayish blue and the ear coverts are a pale bluish green. Cheek patches are green in the male and yellowish green in the female. There is a yellow nuchal collar, and the breast feathers are edged with a darker green. The tail is green above and a dusky yellow below. The bill is orange. Irides are also orange and the legs are bluish

Iris Lorikeets, *Trichoglossus iris*.

gray. Three subspecies are recognized from Timor and Wetar islands in Indonesia.

T. i. iris. The nominate race is as described above and is confined to western Timor.

T. i. rubripileum. This race differs from the nominate by the red on the hindcrown being tinged with green. The band on the hindneck is violet blue and the sides of the head are a light yellowish green. This race comes from the eastern part of the island of Timor.

Varied Lorikeet, _Trichoglossus versicolor_.

T. i. wetterensis. This race differs from the nominate by the sides of the head being darker green and by its larger size. It can be found on the island of Wetar.

The Iris Lorikeet is rare in aviculture and is unlikely ever to be very common. However, it is known that the incubation period is twenty-three days, and the young spend around ten weeks in the nest box before fledging.

Varied Lorikeet
Trichoglossus versicolor

Maximum length is 19cm. Main body plumage is green, which becomes more yellowish on the underparts. The forehead, crown and lores are red, although this is slightly duller in the female. Ear coverts are a greenish yellow, while the throat, cheeks and occiput are green but streaked with yellow. The upper breast is pink streaked with yellow; this is also duller in the female. The mantle and wing coverts are green streaked with yellow. The tail is green. The bill is deep orange. Irides are yellow and the legs are gray. No subspecies are known in this lorikeet, which occurs across northern Australia.

The Varied Lorikeet is rarely seen outside Australia, although reports from Australian aviculturists show that the species is easily kept and bred. The two eggs are normally incubated for twenty-two days, and chicks fledge six weeks later.

In its native New Guinea, the Goldie's Lorikeet, *Trichoglossus goldiei*, is not a numerous species.

Goldie's Lorikeet
Trichoglossus goldiei

Maximum length is 19cm. The main plumage is green, which becomes lighter towards the underparts and the underwing coverts. The forehead and crown are red; this is duller in the female. The occiput is blue, while the cheeks are pinkish purple streaked with blue. The neck is streaked with pale green, while the underparts are streaked with a darker green. A yellow band stretches across the underside of the flight feathers. The tail is olive green above and more yellowish below. The bill is black. Irides are brown and the legs are greenish brown. No subspecies are recognized in this species from New Guinea.

The Goldie's Lorikeet has long been established in aviculture and breeds readily either in aviaries or in inside breeding cages. Incubation takes twenty-four days, with the young fledging about eight weeks later.

Musk Lorikeet, *Glossopsitta concinna*.

The Genus *Glossopsitta*

The genus *Glossopsitta* contains three species; all are found in the southern parts of Australia and two of the three species are also present on Tasmania. As all species in this genus are found only in areas under the jurisdiction of Australia, they are rarely exported and are rare in aviculture. Their wild populations are healthy, however, and there is no threat of habitat destruction which is so common in Indonesian species. Birds of this genus have no erectile crown feathers, and the central tail feathers are pointed. The bill is small, and no sexual dimorphism is present, except very slightly in *G. concinna*, the first species described. Some hybridization has been noted between these species and mainland species of *Trichoglossus*.

Musk Lorikeet
Glossopsitta concinna

Maximum length is 22cm. The main plumage is green, which becomes lighter on the underparts. The forehead and lores are red with a red band extending from the eyes to the sides of the neck. Crown and occiput are blue, which is brighter in the male than in the female. The nape and mantle are brown which is tinted with green. Yellow patches are present on either side of the breast. The underwing coverts are a yellowish green. The tail is green but with reddish orange markings at the bases of lateral feathers. Bill is black tipped with orange. Iris is orange and the legs are a greenish brown. No subspecies are recognized in this lorikeet, which is found in eastern and southeastern Australia.

The Musk Lorikeet, although widely kept and bred within Australia, is rarely seen outside that country. It has been exhibited and bred in England for a number of years at Chester Zoo. The incubation period is twenty-five days, with the young birds staying in the nest box for about eight weeks.

Purple-crowned Lorikeet
Glossopsitta porphyrocephala

Maximum length is 15cm. The forehead is a yellowish orange which darkens to red on the lores.

Ear coverts are a pale orange becoming yellower around the edges. The nape and upper mantle are brown tinted with green. The remainder of the upper parts of the body and head are green. The throat, breast and abdomen are pale blue. There are yellow patches on either side of the breast. Thighs and undertail coverts are yellowish green. Underwing coverts are crimson. The tail is green with reddish orange markings at the base of the lateral feathers. The bill is black. Irides are brown and the legs are gray. No subspecies are recognized in

The Purple-crowned Lorikeet, *Glossopsitta porphyrocephala*.

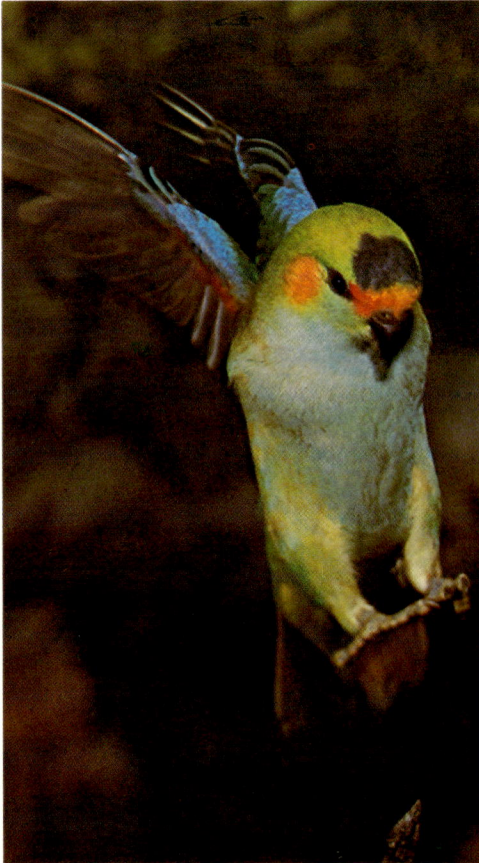

this lorikeet, which can be found in southeastern and southwestern Australia.

This highly attractive lorikeet is again rarely available outside Australia, although it has been widely kept within its own country. The clutch size is unusually large, being of up to five to six eggs. These are incubated for twenty-two days, with the chicks fledging quite early at about six to seven weeks.

Little Lorikeet
Glossopsitta pusilla

Maximum length is 15cm. The main body plumage is green, which becomes lighter and more yellowish on the underparts. The forehead, lores and throat are red. Ear coverts are streaked with pale green. The nape and upper mantle are brown tinted with green. Underwing coverts are a yellowish green. Tail is green with reddish orange markings near the bases of the lateral feathers. The bill is black. Irides are orange to yellow and the legs are a greenish gray. No subspecies are recognized in this lorikeet, which is found in eastern and southeastern Australia.

The Little Lorikeet is virtually unknown outside Australia, and within its own country it is the least well established of the three *Glossopsitta* species. Records show that up to four eggs are laid and are incubated for twenty-three days. The chicks then fledge about seven to eight weeks later.

Little Lorikeet, *Glossopsitta pusilla*.

Papuan Lorikeets *Charmosyna papou goliathina*, the red color phase.

The Genus *Charmosyna*

The genus *Charmosyna* contains thirteen species and so is the largest group of Loriinae. Most species display slight sexual dimorphism and the cere is always naked. There are few other distinctive features of this genus, which is extremely closely related to *Vini*. *Charmosyna* lorikeets prefer a more dilute, runnier nectar mixture than other lories; also, they will not eat the dry nectar products that are for sale. They can also prove sensitive to some of the more acidic fruits often fed to lories; for this genus, the best fruts are generally apple, pear, and pawpaw.

Papuan Lorikeet
Charmosyna papou

The most widely seen race is commonly known as the Stella's Lorikeet. Maximum length is 42cm, of which much is made up of the elongated tail. The main plumage is red. The mantle and wings are dark green. There is a black patch which is streaked with pale blue on the occiput. The rump and upper tail coverts also have blue patches, while the lower flanks and sides of the breast have yellow patches on them. The thighs are black, as is a band which reaches across the abdomen. The under wing coverts are red. The tail is green tipped with yellow above and an orangy yellow below. The bill is orange. Irides are yellowish orange and the legs are also orange. Four subspecies are recognized, coming from New Guinea and Papua New Guinea.

C. p. papou. The nominate race is as described above and is confined to the Vogelkop, Irian Jaya.

C. p. stellae. This race, widely known as the Stella's Lorikeet, differs from the nominate race by the black patch extending from the occiput to the hindneck. There is also no yellow on the lower flanks or the sides of the breast; the lower flanks are black. This race is from the mountains of southeastern New Guinea.

C. p. goliathina. This race, also sometimes known as the Stella's Lorikeet, differs from *C. p. stellae* by the central tail feathers having more yellow towards the tip. There is also a melanistic phase in which the red is replaced by black coloring. This race can be found throughout central New Guinea.

C. p. wahnesi. This race is similar to *C. p. goliathina* but has a wide yellow band across the breast. This race is confined to the Huon Peninsula.

Although the nominate race is rarely seen in captivity, the Stella's Lorikeet *C. p. goliathina* is widely kept, both the normal and melanistic color phases. It appears that the normal color genes are dominant, as red parents will always produce red youngsters, while black, melanistic parents may produce either color types when breeding. Breeding takes place regularly in captivity, with the normal clutch size being two. Incubation takes twenty-six days, and the young spend around eight weeks in the nest box before fledging.

Josephine's Lorikeet
Charmosyna josefinae

Maximum length is 24cm. The main plumage is red. The mantle and wings are dark green, occiput and nape are black, and the rump is blue. The thighs, lower flanks and lower abdomen are a dull black. The underwing coverts are red. The upper tail feathers are red tipped with yellow and yellow on the undersides. The bill is a reddish orange. Irides are yellow and the legs are orange. In the female the lower back is green instead of red. Three subspecies are recognized, all coming from New Guinea.

C. j. josefinae. The nominate race is as described above and is found on the mountains around the Vogelkop, New Guinea.

C. j. sepikiana. This race differs from the nominate by having a wider black abdominal patch. This race is found in western Papua New Guinea.

C. j. cyclopum. This race differs from the nominate by the absence of the black abdominal patch. This race is only found in the mountains of Irian Jaya.

The Josephine's Lorikeet has always been a rarity in aviculture, although now it is becoming established. Reports of incubation time vary, but it normally takes about twenty-five days. The chicks then spend about eight weeks in the nest box before they fledge.

Red-flanked Lorikeet
Charmosyna placentis

Also commonly known as the Pleasing Lorikeet, maximum length is 17cm. There is quite a marked dimorphism between the sexes. In the male the main plumage is green which becomes more yellowish on the underparts. The forehead and forecrown are greenish yellow, while the lores, cheeks and upper throat are a dull red. The ear coverts are violet blue. The underwing coverts, flanks and sides of the breast are red. A yellow band extends across the underside of the flight feathers. The tail is green, tipped with orangy yellow above and yellow below, with a blue patch on the rump. The bill is red. Irides are yellow to orange and the legs are an orange red. The female by

Papuan Lorikeet *Charmosyna papou goliathina*, the melanistic color phase.

In the Red-flanked Lorikeet, *Charmosyna placentis*, sexual dimorphism is marked.

comparison has the forehead and forecrown green. Red markings are replaced by green, and the ear coverts are a dull bluish black and strongly streaked with yellow. Five subspecies are recognized, which come from Indonesia and New Guinea.

C. p. placentis. The nominate race is as described above and can be found on islands of the Moluccas, on Kai and Aru islands and in southern New Guinea.

C. p. intensior. This race differs from the nominate race by being slightly larger, by having a small patch on the blue rump area which is not blue, and by having the forehead more greenish. This race is found on the North Moluccas and on the Western Papuan Islands.

C. p. ornata. This race differs from the nominate by the mantle being a darker green and by the blue rump patch being larger. This race is from the Western Papuan Islands and northwestern New Guinea.

C. p. subplacens. This race differs from the nominate by having no blue patch on the rump. It can be found in eastern New Guinea.

C. p. pallidior. This race is similar to *C. p. subplacens* but with the general plumage being paler, particularly the ear coverts in the male. This race can be found on Woodlark Island and throughout the Bismarck Archipelago, to the Admiralty and Nuguria islands.

The Red-flanked, or Pleasing, Lorikeet is, as the latter common name suggests, one of the most beautiful and charming of all Loriinae species to keep. It has never become very widely established, possibly because of the delicacy of newly imported birds, which need delicate care, but once established they often breed willingly and are much at home in inside breeding cages. Incubation takes twenty-five days and the young stay in the nest box for seven to eight weeks.

Striated Lorikeet
Charmosyna multistriata

Maximum length is 18cm. The main plumage is green, which becomes more yellowish on the forehead, throat and sides of the head. The hindcrown and nape are brown, with the nape being

spotted with yellow. The breast is
a darker green and is streaked
with yellow. The neck and lower
underparts are a lighter green
which is also streaked with yellow. The vent is red. The tail is
olive green tipped with yellow
above and yellow below. The bill is
gray tipped with orange on the
upper mandible, while the lower
mandible is completely orange.
The irides are red and the legs are
a bluish gray. No subspecies are
recognized in this lorikeet which
comes from western New Guinea.

The Striated Lorikeet is not
frequently seen in captivity; however the limited information available on the breeding habits of this
lorikeet suggests that their eggs
take 28 days to hatch and that
the young then spend up to 8
weeks in the nest before fledging.

Wilhelmina's Lorikeet
Charmosyna wilhelminae

Maximum length is 13cm. The
main plumage is green, which
becomes more yellowish on the
underparts. The crown and nape
are purplish brown, with the nape
being streaked with blue. The
lower back is red, with the rump
being dark purple. The breast is
streaked with yellow. Underwing
coverts are red with a red band
running across the underside of
the flight feathers. The tail is
green marked with red. The bill is
orange; irides are orange to red
and the legs are gray. Females
differ by having the lower back

Fairy Lorikeet *Charmosyna pulchella pulchella*.

green and lacking the red band across the underside of the flight feathers. No subspecies are recognized in this lorikeet that is found in the highlands of New Guinea.

The Wilhelmina's Lorikeet is again little known in captivity, and little information is available on its breeding. Incubation takes 23 days.

Fairy Lorikeet
Charmosyna pulchella

Maximum length is 18cm. The main plumage is red. The back, wings and tail coverts are dark green. The rump is dark blue. Thighs and nuchal patch are dark purple. There are yellow streaks on the breast and sometimes on the lower flanks. Underwing coverts are green and red. The tail is green at the base, becoming red and yellow towards the tip above, and the underside is bright yellow. The bill is orangy red. Irides are yellowish orange and the legs are a light orange. The female can be identified by also having yellow patches on the sides of the rump. Two subspecies are recognized, both from New Guinea.

C. p. pulchella. The nominate race is as described above and is found throughout New Guinea.

C. p. rothschildi. This race differs from the nominate by the presence of a large green breast patch with yellow streaking. It also has a purple black abdomen and the rump is green. This race is restricted to the mountain ranges of Irian Jaya.

The Fairy Lorikeet is well known in aviculture, with both races being seen, although the nominate is by far the more common. These birds thrive best in tropical houses or inside breeding cages but can live outside in warm countries if care is taken in regards to temperature and the freshness of its food. Breeding has taken place but not yet regularly. Incubation is twenty-five days and the chicks take about nine weeks to fledge.

Palm Lorikeet
Charmosyna palmarum

Maximum length is 17cm. The main plumage is green, which is paler and more yellowish on the underparts. The chin, lores and area around the base of the bill are red. The mantle is tinged with olive brown. The underwing coverts are grayish green. The tail feathers are green, with the central feathers heavily tipped with yellow; the outer ones are also tipped but less prominently. The bill is orange. Irides are yellow and the legs are orangy yellow. The female often has less, if any, red on the chin. No subspecies are recognized in this lorikeet, which originates from the Bank Islands and Santa Cruz and also from what used to be the New Hebrides.

The Palm Lorikeet is virtually unknown in aviculture and no information is available on its breeding.

Fairy Lorikeets of the subspecies *Charmosyna pulchella rothschildi*.

Meek's Lorikeet
Charmosyna meeki

Maximum length is 16cm. The main plumage is green, which is more yellowish on the underparts and underwing coverts. The crown is dull blue. The mantle is strongly tinged with olive brown, and the sides of the neck are light green with darker streaking. There is a light yellow band reaching across the underside of the secondaries. The tail is dark green tipped with yellow above and bright yellow below. The bill is orange. Irides are yellowish orange and the legs are also orange. No subspecies are recognized in this lorikeet that occurs on the Solomon Islands.

The Meek's Lorikeet is unknown in aviculture and no information is available on its breeding.

Red-chinned Lorikeet
Charmosyna rubrigularis

Also known as the Red-marked Lorikeet. Maximum length is 17cm. The plumage is mainly green, which becomes more yellowish on the underparts. The chin and the base of the lower mandible are red, giving the bird its common names. The lores are green. The underwing coverts are a yellowish green, and a yellow band reaches across the underside of the flight feathers. The tail is green tipped with yellow above and a dusky yellow below. The bill is a reddish orange. The irides and legs are a lighter orange. No subspecies are recognized in this lorikeet that comes from the Bismarck Archipelago and islands off the northeastern coast of New Guinea.

This species is also little known in captivity, with no information available on its breeding.

Red-throated Lorikeet
Charmosyna amabilis

Also known as the Golden-banded Lorikeet. Maximum length is 18cm. The plumage is mostly green, which is paler on the underparts and underwing coverts. The ear coverts are streaked with a bluish green. The lores, cheeks and throat are red. The throat has a narrow yellow line running below and bordering the red. The thighs are dark red. The tail is green tipped with yellow above and yellow below. The bill is orange. Irides are yellow and the legs are orange. No subspecies are recognized in this lorikeet which inhabits the Fiji Islands.

This species is unknown in captivity and is probably close to

extinction in the wild. No information is available on its breeding.

Red-spotted Lorikeet
Charmosyna rubronotata

Maximum length is 17cm. The plumage is mainly green, which is paler on the underparts. The forehead and forecrown are red. Ear coverts are purplish blue with lighter streaking. The spots from which the bird gets its common name are present on the sides of the breast, upper tail coverts and underwing coverts. There is a yellow band across the underside of the secondaries. The tail is green above and yellow below. The bill is red. Irides are orange and the legs are red. The female differs from the male by her forehead and forecrown being green instead of red; her ear coverts are also green. Two subspecies are recognized in this lorikeet from New Guinea, Salawati and the Biak Islands.

C. r. rubronotata. The nominate race is as described above and is found on Salawati and in northwestern New Guinea.

C. r. kordoana. This race differs from the nominate by the red of the crown being paler and more extensive. This race is restricted to the Biak Islands.

The nominate race of the Red-spotted Lorikeet has become established in aviculture in the space of the last five years, having by now been bred in several collections. It is known that incu-

Papuan Lorikeet *Charmosyna papou goliathina* at eighteen days of age.

bation takes 23 days and that the chicks fledge at around 8 weeks of age.

Duchess Lorikeet
Charmosyna margarethae

Maximum length is 20cm. The main plumage is red. The wings, back and undertail coverts are green. The rump and upper tail coverts are an olive green, but the sides of the rump are red. The hindcrown and occiput are purple black. There is a broad yellow band across the breast, continuing as a narrow band on the mantle; this yellow is bordered above by a narrow purple black line. The lower abdomen is marked with a dull purple. The tail is red tipped with yellow. The bill is orange. Irides are yellowish orange and the legs are also orange. No subspecies are recognized in this lorikeet that inhabits Bougainville Island and the Solomon Islands.

The Duchess Lorikeet is virtually unknown in aviculture and no information is available about its breeding.

Blue-fronted Lorikeet
Charmosyna toxopei

Maximum length is 16cm. The plumage is mainly green, which is more yellowish on the underparts. The forehead is green. The forecrown is blue, though this is fainter and less extensive on the female. The chin and throat are greenish yellow, and there is a yellow band reaching across the underside of the secondaries; this is more distinct in the female. The tail is green, slightly tipped with yellow above and yellow marked with orange below. The bill is orange. Irides are yellowish orange and the legs are a reddish orange. No subspecies are recognized in this lorikeet, which is confined to the island of Buru in Indonesia.

The Blue-fronted Lorikeet is unknown in aviculture and is probably the most endangered species described in this book. Its future is extremely uncertain and it is unlikely ever to appear in captivity.

The nominate subspecies of the Papuan Lorikeet, *Charmosyna papou*.

The Genus *Oreopsittacus*

The genus *Oreopsittacus* contains only one species, although it is unique in having fourteen tail feathers whereas all other parrot species have twelve. This species is small and slim, resembling species of *Charmosyna*.

Arfak Alpine Lorikeet *Oreopsittacus arfaki*

Also known as the Blue-cheeked Alpine, or Whiskered, Lorikeet. The maximum length is 15cm. There is some sexual dimorphism in this species. The main body plumage is green, which becomes more yellowish on the underparts. The lores and cheeks are purple with a double row of white spots streaked above the purple cheeks. In male birds the forehead and crown are red, while in the females the same area is green. The abdomen and lower flanks are reddish orange. The sides of the breast and underwing coverts are red. There is also a yellow band across the underside of the secondaries. The tail is green tipped with red above, and the underside is red with some yellow on the sides of the undertail coverts. The bill is black. The iris is dark brown and the legs are greenish gray. Three subspecies are recognized, all coming from the mountains of New Guinea.

O. a. arfaki. The nominate race is as described above and is found in the mountains of the Vogelkop, Irian Jaya.

O. a. major. This race differs from the nominate by being slightly larger and by the tips of the tail being scarlet. It is confined to the region of the Snow Mountains, Irian Jaya.

O. a. grandis. This race is similar to *O. a. major* but differs by the abdomen and lower flanks being green. This race is from southeastern New Guinea.

Unfortunately, this species is practically unknown in aviculture and few observations have been made in the wild. A limited number of these birds have been imported in the last few years, but these have proved difficult to establish in captivity and no breeding has yet taken place.

The Musschenbroek's Lorikeet, *Neopsittacus musschenbroekii*.

The Genus *Neopsittacus*

The genus *Neopsittacus* contains two species; both are small-bodied lorikeets with long tails. The main feature of this genus, in comparison to *Charmosyna* or *Oreopsittacus*, is the broader and more heavily built bill.

Musschenbroek's Lorikeet *Neopsittacus musschenbroekii*

Maximum length is 23cm. The main plumage is green, which becomes more yellowish towards the underparts. The crown and nape are olive brown and streaked with yellow. The hindneck is also olive brown, and the lores are a dull greenish black. The cheeks are dull brown and streaked with green. The throat, breast and center of the abdomen are red, as are the underwing coverts and a broad band which reaches across the underside of the flight feathers. The central tail feathers are green tipped with yellow, as are the lateral feathers, but these are also variably marked with red. The underside is a bright yellowish orange. The bill is pale yellow. Irides are red and the legs are

gray. Two subspecies are recognized in this lorikeet, both originating from New Guinea.

N. m. musschenbroekii. The nominate race is as described above and is confined to the mountains of the Vogelkop, Irian Jaya.

N. m. major. This race differs from the nominate race by being larger and by the streaking on the cheeks being less green and more yellowish. This race is found in the Snow Mountains, Irian Jaya, and throughout the mountains of southeastern New Guinea. The population from the Snow Mountains was previously treated as a separate race, *N. m. medius,* but is now considered to be *N. m. major.*

The Musschenbroek's Lorikeet is established in aviculture but is still considered a rarity and commands a high price. Breeding does however take place regularly. The eggs are incubated for twenty-five days and the chicks spend around seven weeks in the nest box before fledging.

Emerald Lorikeet *Neopsittacus pullicauda*

This species is rarely seen but

is superficially very similar to Musschenbroek's Lorikeet. It can be distinguished though by the following features: smaller size; more orangish bill; little or no brown marking; and no yellow tips to the tail feathers.

Maximum length is 18cm. The main plumage is green, which becomes more yellowish on the underparts. The crown and nape are slightly streaked with yellowish green. The nape is also slightly tinged with olive brown. Lores are a dull greenish black. The cheeks are green, slightly streaked with yellow. The throat, breast and center of the abdomen are bright red. The underwing coverts and a broad band across the underside of the flight feathers are also red. The tail is green marked with red above and a dull olive green below. The bill is orange. Irides are red and the legs are gray. Three subspecies are recognized, all from the mountains of New Guinea.

N. p. pullicauda. The nominate race is as described above and is found throughout the mountain ranges of southeastern New Guinea.

N. p. alpinus. This race differs from the nominate race by having a lighter, more orangish red on the abdomen. It also has a darker green on the upper parts of the body. It is found in the Snow Mountains.

N. p. socialis. This race is similar to the nominate race but has a darker green on the sides of the head. It also has less olive brown on the nape. This race can be found only in the Herzog Mountains of New Guinea.

The Emerald Lorikeet is only fairly recently starting to appear in aviculture, despite being locally common in the wild. As yet no captive breeding information is available; however, as it is extremely closely related to the Musschenbroek's Lorikeet it is likely to behave similarly while breeding.

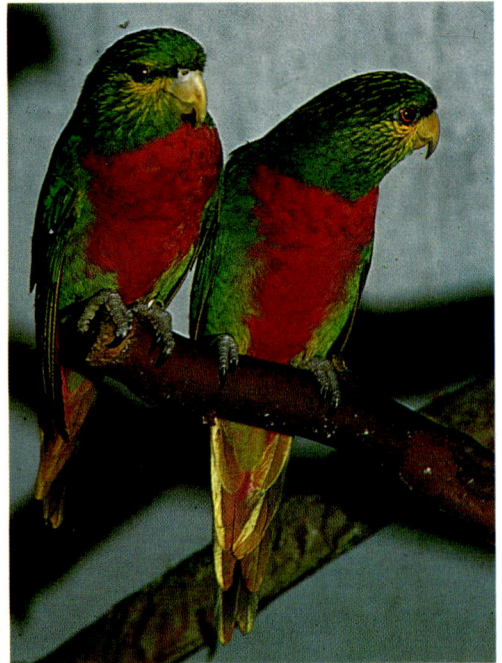

Emerald Lorikeets, *Neopsittacus pullicauda*. Sexual dimorphism does not occur in this genus.

Glossary

ASCARIDS: A group of roundworm-like parasites common in Australasian and Asian psittacines.

AVICULTURE: The pastime of keeping and breeding birds in captivity.

AVITAMINOSIS: Any disease caused by a lack of certain vitamins from a diet. E.g, avitaminosis-A is a lack of vitamin A in the diet.

BEND OF THE WING: Area along the front top of the wing, covered by lesser wing coverts.

CANDLING: Using an artificial light source to view development inside the egg.

CERE: The fleshy area around the nostrils, covered with feathers in some species and bare in others.

CROP: A thin-walled area of the lower esophagus which can swell to hold food until the stomach empties, or, alternatively, until it is needed for feeding chicks by regurgitation.

CROWN: Area around the center of the top of the head.

DRY-BULB THERMOMETER: The instrument for measuring temperature inside the incubator.

EMBRYO: The early stages of a chick's development within the egg.

FECES: Waste matter from the gut, which exits the body via the large intestines and cloaca.

FERAL: Term give to domestic forms that have become established as wild populations.

FLEDGLING: A young bird that had just fledged, or left the nest.

FORENECK: Area above the breast and just below the throat.

GENUS: A group of birds sharing common physical characteristics which make them distinct from other groups of birds.

INCUBATOR: Container for artificially incubating eggs.

INITIAL INTERNAL PIP: The moment the chick starts to push up to and against the membrane between itself and the air sac inside the egg.

IRIS: The colored region of the eye.

LAPAROSCOPE: A surgical instrument used widely in avian medicine, often used to sex birds.

LORES: Area between the eye and the beak.

LORIINAE: Subfamily of Psittaciformes containing eleven genera, encompassing all species of lories and lorikeets.

MANDIBLE: Name given to the two parts (upper and lower) of the bill.

MANTLE: The area between the hindneck and shoulders, down to the upper back.

MITES: Small arachnid parasites that can infest captive populations of birds.

MONOMORPHIC: Birds in which there are no easily identifiable differences between males and females.

NAPE: Area at the back of the neck.

NECROSIS: Areas of dead tissue on a live animal.

NOMINATE: Term given to the first subspecies (race) to be described.

NUCHAL: The area between the nape and hindneck.

OCCIPUT: Area on the back of the head just above the nape.

PIP: Term used to describe the chick breaking though the egg shell.

PRIMARIES: The outside ten wing feathers that give a birds its main flying power.

QUARANTINE: A period of isolation to ensure that a bird is not carrying an infectious disease.

RACE: Commonly used term meaning *subspecies.*

RUMP: Area above the base of the tail.

SCAPULARS: Feathers running down the back against the inner edge of the wing.

SECONDARIES: The ten inner wing
  feathers.
SEXUAL DIMORPHISM: Noticeable visible
  differences between the sexes in a
  bird species.
SPECIES: Distinct member of a genus.
SUBSPECIES: Distinct member of a
  species.
VENT: External orifice of the cloaca.
WET-BULB THERMOMETER: Instrument
  used to determine the level of
  humidity in an incubator.

Lory Societies

Below are the addresses of societies in America, Australia, and Europe which may be of use to anyone contemplating keeping lories or lorikeets.

International Loriinae Society, 8023
  17th N.E., Seattle, WA 98115,
  U.S.A.
American Federation of Aviculture,
  PO Box 56218, Phoenix, AZ 85079,
  U.S.A.
National Parrot Association, 8 N.
  Hoffman Lane, Hauppaugue, NY
  11788, U.S.A.
Avicultural Advancement Council of
  Canada, PO Box 5126, Station B,
  Victoria, BC, Canada.
Parrot Society of Australia, PO Box
  75, Salisbury Q1D 4107, Australia.
The Avicultural Society, c/o Bristol
  Zoo, Clifton, Bristol BS8 3HA, U.K.
The Parrot Society, 108b Fenlake
  Road, Bedford MK42 0EU, U.K.
Foreign Bird Federation, 6 Elms
  Grove, Old Arley, Coventry, U.K.
Foreign Bird League, Monks Cottage,
  58 Preston Crowmarsh, Benson,
  Oxon OX9 6SL, U.K.

Selected Bibliography

Arnall, L. and Keymer, I.F. 1975. *Bird Diseases.* T.F.H Publications, New Jersey, U.S.A.

Beehler, B. M., Pratt, T.K., and Zimmerman, D. 1986. *Birds of New Guinea.* Princeton University Press, New Jersey, U.S.A.

Du Pont, J. 1971. *Philippine Birds.* Delaware Museum of Natural History, U.S.A.

Forshaw, J. 1973. *Parrots of the World.* T.F.H. Publications, New Jersey, U.S.A.

Fowler, M. 1986. *Zoo and Wild Animal Medicine.* W. B. Saunders Company, Philadelphia, U.S.A.

Harvey, R. 1990. *Practical Incubation.* Birdworld, Farnham, U.K.

Low, R. 1977. *Lories and Lorikeets.* Paul Elek, London.

Low, R. 1980. *Parrots: Their Care and Breeding.* Blandford Press, Dorset, England.

Pizzey, G. 1980. *A Field Guide to the Birds of Australia.* William Collins and Sons, Sydney, Australia.

Pratt, H. D. , Bruner, P. L., and Berrett, D. G. 1987. *The Birds of Hawaii and the Tropical Pacific.* Princeton University Press, New Jersey, U.S.A.

Rutgers, A. and Norris, K. A. 1977. *Encyclopaedia of Aviculture.* Blandford Press, Dorset, England.

Silva, T. 1989. *A Monograph of Endangered Parrots.* Silvio Mattacchione & Co., Pickering, Ontario, Canada.

Watling, D. 1982. *Birds of Fiji, Tonga, and Samoa.* Princeton University Press, New Jersey, U.S.A.

Woolham, F. 1987. *The Handbook of Aviculture.* Blandford Press, Dorset, England.

INDEX

Page numbers in **boldface** refer to illustrations.